*Bound Yet Free*

# *Bound Yet Free*

## 52-Week Devotional for Those Bound Seeking Freedom

### Jennifer Kelly
(a Georgia State Inmate)

Copyright @2020 Jennifer Kelly

All rights reserved. No part of this book may be used or reproduced by any means, graphic, electronic, or mechanical, including photocopying, recording, taping or by any information storage retrieval system without the written permission of the publisher except in the case of brief quotations embodies in critical articles and reviews.

ISBN: 9798615019180 (sc)

Unless otherwise noted, Scripture quotations are taken from the New King James Version*.© 1982 by Thomas Nelson. Used by permission. All rights reserved.

All other scripture references are from the following sources:
The Holy Bible, New International Version* (NIV). © 1984 by the International Bible Society. Used by permission. All rights reserved. Holman Christian Standard Bible* (HCSB). © 1999, 2000, 2002, 2003, 2009 Holman Bible Publishers. Holman Christian Standard Bible®, Holman CSB®, and HCSB® are federally registered trademarks of Holman Bible Publishers. Used by permission. All rights reserved.

Printed in the United States of America

## *Acknowledgments*

If anyone in the entire universe has reason to be thankful, it is certainly me. God has blessed me beyond measure, and I love and appreciate Him. I've been out of His will and been guilty of innumerable acts of disobedience; however, I've always prayed and always thanked Him. God will not find it a surprise that I thank Him for giving me the opportunity to write this devotional with hopes of letting any who make use of it to be blessed and drawn to Him. I thank you, Father, that when this prodigal ran from You, Your feet ran towards me with open arms.

My Grandmother (Charlie Mae Mills) - I am sure you are part of Heaven's cloud of witnesses and I thank you for your love and wisdom you imparted into my life. You weren't rich or educated, but you will always be considered the wisest woman that ever crossed my path. Mother, I love you and forever will.

My Mother (Vera L. Williams) - Thank you for giving me all that you had to offer. You've given to me financially, you've given me much time on your knees, and I'm sure you gave me many hours of your sleep. Thank you for your prayers. I know I've troubled your spirit more than you'll ever tell me.

My Father (John Henry Spann)- You have gone on to glory, and I await the day we reunite. Daddy, you are the one who taught me prayer.

No one can take those images from my heart and mind praying with me and my sister on Sunday mornings.

My Siblings (Julie Gordon, JoAnn Baker, John "Jeff" Spann, and Darwin Williams) – Thank you for your kindness whenever we were together. Distance and different lifestyles may have kept us apart for years, but whenever we were together we always had fun. Thank you for always treating my children with much love. I love you guys. I also thank my brother-in-law, Greg Gordon (Julie's husband,) for accepting me from day one and being the most humble genuine encourager I've met in years. I love you.

Lisa Mahaffey – When I first met you, you were known to me as "Miss Lisa". You are a dynamic lady. You came into my life and many other ladies' lives as a Bible study teacher in the Fayette County Jail. You exuded the warmth and love of God as a blanket covers one freezing in a house with no heat. I looked forward to your visit every week. You taught the Word of God in layman's terms, and your ears were attentive to our cries and questions. The prison has an email system for friends and family to stay connected, and once I got in the prison system and received the state-issued tablet, my first email was from you, Miss Lisa, with a great lesson on Samson. You have been a constant in my life for the past year and a half, and I'll always love you. God used you mightily in the fulfillment of one of my dreams – the publishing of this book. I know in my heart of hearts that we've just begun. You typed, edited, asked questions for clarity, researched to find doors to make it happen, and even participated in a webinar for me. Your prayers and encouragement have carried me on some of the most lonesome days I experienced. You are a treasure that I'm forever glad I found. I can't just thank you alone because your counterpart, your husband Mike, was a part of it all the way to the end. Sir, my hat is off to you for sharing your jewel of a wife with me and many other ladies behind the walls. Miss Lisa, you started out as my Bible study teacher and now you're a genuine friend. I know our paths crossed for a reason and this is not the end of "us." I love you and we will soon rejoice and praise God together. Thanks for not giving up on me. Thanks for showing me that God hasn't given up on me either. I also thank your son, Clark Mahaffey, for helping with the book's layout. Clark, you came home from college to spend time with your parents (the Mahaffeys) and you ended up joining the bandwagon to help a prisoner you never met – a prisoner whose lifestyle was so different from yours. You could have run, but because of the Godly example of your parents and your heart, you helped. I thank you and trust God for your future to shine brighter than you can imagine.

    The Women at Pulaski State Prison – I give a shout out to you and many of the staff members. I especially thank God for Anitra Hicks. If ever God used a young woman to make me walk in forgiveness and to be patient, it was you, Neet. I truly love you and pray for your success beyond prison.

Amazon – Lastly but definitely not last, I thank Amazon for paving the way and opening doors for first time broke authors. No wonder you're number one in your field.

All Others – I could go on and on with thanking people that blessed me on my sordid path. If your name is not included, it's a head thing, not a heart thing. I love too many to count.

# *Foreword*

As I sit here looking at this devotional book ready to go to print, I feel the emotions welling up in me. What God has done in and through the life of Jennifer Kelly is amazing and awe-inspiring, and God allowed me to have a cat-bird seat to it all. As a clergy volunteer at the Fayette County Jail in Fayette County, Georgia, I met Jennifer Kelly in November 2018 following her arrest for shoplifting.

 Jennifer was a faithful attendee for six months to the weekly Bible study I facilitated before leaving to serve her prison sentence. I got to know her heart and some of her background, but it wasn't until she arrived at Pulaski State Prison that I had access to an email system to communicate with her daily. Our relationship began to grow deeper where Jennifer opened up about the struggles she has faced in her life and her desire to overcome, walk in God's ways, and make amends for all the damage she has done to others in her life.

 Like the apostle Paul, God began using Jennifer to share His word with others in the prison who otherwise would never have heard the good news of Jesus Christ. Jennifer was a willing vehicle and obedient to what God had in store for her. I truly believe she was a magnet others in the prison were drawn to because she always had this joyous smile on her face. Jennifer radiated happiness whenever I was around her, and it was infectious.

Jennifer asked me to send her some composition notebooks, and to my surprise, one day she told me she had used one to write 52 weeks worth of devotions. She knew I had published a book years ago and asked me for help in publishing hers. When I received the entire hand-written manuscript in the mail and began to read it, I was blown away. Her writing was so heartfelt and beautifully written. She so inspired me that I knew I had to make her dream a reality.

I typed up sections of the book and then cut and pasted them into the J-Pay email system so Jennifer could edit for clarity. Jennifer even had me hunt down the courtroom transcript because the judge's words were very powerful to her which she wanted to include. I cannot wait for Jennifer to see this book in print along with her family, other inmates currently incarcerated with her, as well as the judge who sentenced her.

Where God takes it from here, only He knows. There are many broken and bound people in this world just waiting to be set free. With God, all things are possible, and I believe He has a plan to use Jennifer's inspiring devotions to change lives. I'm just thankful to have been given the privilege to watch God transform a life and then use it to multiply with ripple effects wherever this book lands.

*Lisa Mahaffey*

## *Isaiah 61:1-3*

The Spirit of the Lord God is upon me; because the Lord hath anointed me to preach good tidings unto the meek; he hath sent me to bind up the brokenhearted, to proclaim liberty to the captives, and the opening of the prison to them that are bound; To proclaim the acceptable year of the Lord, and the day of vengeance of our God; to comfort all that mourn; To appoint unto them that mourn in Zion, to give unto them beauty for ashes, the oil of joy for mourning, the garment of praise for the spirit of heaviness; that they might be called trees of righteousness, the planting of the Lord, that he might be glorified.

## Back Story

My name is Jennifer Kelly, and at the time of this publishing, I sit in Georgia's Pulaski State Prison. I wanted to share a little bit about myself and my journey and what brought me to the point of writing a devotional book.

In my day, we dreamed of big homes, a family, possibly a pet, but definitely the white picket fence. I remember growing up in a very nice crime-free neighborhood. I had a two-parent family, one with my mom and dad, and then with my mom and stepdad. There were four children in my family. My eldest sister and brother lived with my grandparents while my baby sister and I were raised together in what I'll always describe as the white picket fence family home.

I never recall going to bed hungry, living with disconnected utilities, or wearing clothes that would get us picked on. I have great memories of laughter with my mom and dad. My fondest memories go back to Sunday mornings, where we had this stereo in our living room that my mom played gospel music on pretty loud. I'm sure many younger people reading this will not know that 8-track tape players were big gaudy versions of CD's. Daddy taught my sister and me to pray, kneeling down with us in his bedroom.

Momma would be preparing Sunday breakfast and dinner simultaneously. These were the days where God began planting the seeds of prayer in my heart. We were a church-going family. I have to say both my parents were honest people. They worked for what they had and had no parts in illegal activities. I remember them telling us, "if you get in trouble defending yourselves, we'll be there for you, but if it's for stealing and costs one cent to free you, we aren't coming." They always taught us to work hard.

To be on the outside looking in at my life, you'd think all was great and would be that way forever. I was an "A" student, and I wanted to stand out. I was happy for a while until my parents did the unthinkable and got divorced, making me extremely angry. While my dad moved all his things out, I remember going to my grandmother's house, and when my mom, sister, and I returned home, Daddy was gone. I misdirected my anger at my mom for unknown reasons. Looking back now, I have a different perspective and realize all the anger I carried for years was uncalled for and faulty. A few years before my Daddy passed away, he confessed to my siblings and me that he had quite a few infidelities. Though my dad has since passed away and there was pain in my life caused by the divorce, I will never forget that my dad was the one who introduced me to prayer, which was a gift I was blessed to receive.

Following my parent's divorce, Momma remarried, which I didn't like. I grew to pretend I was happy and repress my emotions. Momma's new husband was the first felon I ever knew. Momma made sure church was a part of our lives, and we were active in our local church, where I did numerous speaking engagements on behalf of our youth department, sang in the choir with Momma, and served as an usher. I heard the gospel, but I can't recall ever hearing about the grace and mercy of God. Maybe it was preached, but it didn't leave an impression on me enough to remember.

My stepdad opened the door to alcohol in our household. I had relatives who drank, but I don't recall liquor ever being in our household before. Even though I remember many things from my past, my family seems to have mentally buried those things, don't remember, or don't want to discuss them- and today I get it.

Home became a place where I frequently saw violence, endured molestation, and experienced verbal abuse because of my weight. I had no self-esteem. I felt rejected, forsaken, and nasty. I left home as a teenager at the age of 16, which I do not recommend for any young person thinking it will bring freedom because it doesn't. Stealing became a normal part of my life. The streets have no love for you - believe me. I learned to do the best I could as a drop out teen, but I never called my dad or any other family members for help.

Broken-hearted, my dad came looking for his runaway daughter whom he loved, and in my shame and fear thinking his motive was to "fuss me out," I hid from my father relying on friends to tell him I was not there. Why did I hide? Years later, I thought about the foolishness of that action. My Daddy sought me out like God seeks His beloved children, and I did like many of us do today – I ran.

I ended up being a live trickster. I didn't feel loved, and I had none to give. Men came into my life only to leave. I stole their money and any valuables they possessed. They stole from me in my eyes. I did not want sex and made many excuses for years not to perform, but I had needs they could meet like housing and food, so I reluctantly returned the favors. As I got older, my bitterness and anger of things done to me in my childhood led me to retaliate, but the things I did only caused me to endure consequences. Because of my reckless choices, my head was sought on a platter more times than I can count, but God had plans for me, which would involve taking me off the shelf one day and using me for His glory, so He never allowed anyone to take me out.

One night at a local bar, I met a man whom I started a real relationship with, or at least I thought, and from that relationship came my first child. I felt accepted by his family, and we were committed to going to church on Sundays even after long nights of partying on the weekends. I had my own little family and fully expected I'd be marching down the aisle with my love. I was on cloud nine until the aftershocks of the truth came to light. Not only was he married, but also, he was an ordained minister. I asked myself where God was in all of this. I stayed until my child was over a year old, and then I disappeared.

I finally left my hometown of Albany, Georgia, and began moving from state to state. I opened myself up to drugs, more thievery, clubbing, and every type of sin imaginable. For some odd reason, I always ran into people doing some type of scheme, and I'd jump on board. In 1992, I had my first run-in with the law, arrested for the sale and delivery of cocaine. After being released on bond and having some serious talks with acquaintances, I relocated to upstate New York, where I met my husband, a man who really loved me. At the time, I didn't comprehend that love, I just wanted someone to take care of me. I was an empty shell of a woman. My husband worked and did no illegal activities simply wanting to love and settle down. Everything God offers, I sought in a man like security and stability, but without Christ, it is like an elephant walking on thin, thin ice. It is IMPOSSIBLE. It is also unfair to the one you seek it from.

We lived a lowkey life because there was an active warrant for me for skipping bond in my cocaine arrest. Not a soul in my new circle knew but me. I went to church, but I still partied with my new friends without my husband. He did not partake but allowed me to do whatever I wanted. I called this disorderly life a blessed life, and I even had my second blessing of a child yet continued in this unwholesome lifestyle.

In 1995, we relocated back to my hometown of Albany, and for a few months, all looked well. Birds of a feather do flock together, and we have a tendency to find our kind. I began shoplifting for a living; sad, foolish, so selfish and true. My second arrest came in February 1996 for shoplifting in Albany, GA. Dumb and embarrassed were the only words I can think of to describe where I was in life. Albany was home and where my respectable family lived. Everywhere I went in the jail, I was referred to as "Mrs. Williams' daughter." I was an embarrassment to my family. I was sentenced to one year in the penitentiary and even transported back to Florida to face the cocaine charges I ran from. The Florida charges were dropped, but I did Georgia's entire year.

Prison is where I began to see the Lord for myself. It's awful to say, but I learned God's truths while incarcerated yet didn't yield to His ways once released. But that didn't stop God from pursuing me. God spoke to me and gave me revelations in His word, and during time served at Washington State Prison in Milledgeville, GA, I remember this conversation between me and God:

Me: Lord, what would you have me to do?
God: Share the gospel.
Me: I'm not going to preach. (but in my spirit the word "evangelist" kept sounding in my spirit which the dictionary defines as travelling minister. So, I placed a fleece before God and said...)
Me: God if you mean for me to be a vessel to share the gospel, fix it so I can be ordained before I leave prison.

Within 48 hours God showed me who He is. I was in the prison yard talking to a group of ladies when a young lady walked up and said, "If any of you ladies know someone here that is called by God to share the gospel, tell them to see me for the ordination process." I stood there in awe and followed through with her becoming ordained. My spirit was rejoicing, and I wanted the world to know. I sent copies to all my family hoping for them to be proud of me, but no one accepted me as God's messenger. I have never shared the gospel in the "free world". I have only shared the gospel in my "normal" setting – prison/jail. I had not learned the concept of you obey God to please Him even if no one accepts you. I had not understood the power of Paul's ministry fully who waited on no man to approve him. Approval was the greatest desire of mine for years; my family's approval. I didn't care what other people in the world said.

I got out of prison in February 1997 and got pregnant again having my second daughter in October 1998. I cannot count the times I've lived in penal facilities since then. For a while, I walked as a productive citizen, and I was a wife I suppose. Next, I became pregnant with my baby boy, Donald Jr. He had the eyes of a saint to me. You'd think that my love for my only beloved son would have motivated me to stay straight, but that is not how addiction works. There are families that may never understand the criminal behavior and the addiction coupled together. The violator doesn't even understand. There were extended periods where I went to church with my children. I read the Bible with them, taught them scriptures, and participated in church events, but inconsistency was always the issue. I was too broken to give them all they needed, but thankfully God brought them through despite my weaknesses.

At the writing of this book, it's 2020 and I've starved for what God had in His hands and heart to give me for years. What God has is not counterfeit love. He is LOVE, and even in my unfaithfulness, His love never faltered. He never forsook such a wretch as me. Where I felt forsaken and unacceptable, He gave me His gift of salvation and His presence. In the dark shameful recesses of my heart, He shone His light and filled every crevice.

Today, I still don't feel totally accepted by those I desire acceptance from, but I have received Jesus' acceptance, and in Him, I am able to go forward.

I'm presently on my last prison sentence ever! Some people say, "never say never," but when you know without a doubt the transformation God has done in your heart, you can say it with confidence. This prison sentence is my personal exodus. Moses had to be placed in the river and "drawn out" as part of God's plan and purpose for his life, the Israelites had to be "drawn out" of their bondage to the wilderness on their journey to their promised land, so why can't I believe I'm on my exodus from the clutches of that dragon, Satan, who has held me in captivity for years?

I'm ashamed of many things I've done and of things done to me, But I'm grateful God snatched me out of many fires and didn't let the devil have victory in my life. The devil has lost and, in spite of it all, I'm free today and my future will definitely be better than my former days. I am slowly but surely getting it. I am more than the devastating acts I did or were done to me. I'm in Him – I'm free! Hallelujah, hallelujah, hallelujah!

The Introduction following in the next section outlines the day I was sentenced to my final prison stay on March 22, 2019.

## Introduction

On March 22, 2019, I did what I'd done numerous times before – face a Superior Court judge. I was in Fayette County, Georgia, to make a guilty plea "deal" for a 10-year sentence with five years to serve and the option of parole. The district attorney and my public defender were in total agreement with this "mercy" sentence. I was not willingly on board, but my extensive record spoke for itself.

The Honorable Judge Ballard was on the bench known by inmates to be a pretty fair man. I'm standing at the podium ready to agree to a sentence I was very much opposed to when Judge Ballard shook my socks off. He had called me to come forth so he could discuss my options. The following is our conversation straight from the transcript.

*Fayetteville, Fayette County, Georgia; March 22. 2019, in open court.)*

THE COURT: *Come to the podium, please, Ms. Kelly.*

*Okay. Ms. Kelly, you've been brought in for arraignment, and that's your opportunity to plead guilty or not guilty to the charges; and you have just signed a document saying that you plead not guilty.*

*And what that does is, it joins the issue in the case, and we go – our next step will be to have a trial in this matter. And that's going to be your right. You can have an opportunity to have a jury trial if you choose to do so.*

*Of course, you and your lawyer can have discussions with the State to talk about some type of plea. What I want you to know is that you have no less than 12 felony convictions on your criminal history. It's 62 pages long.*

*These shopliftings that you're charged with – and you're charged with two in this current case – are felonies. You could receive 20 years in prison. You could be sentenced – if indictments were formed and.... -- the way to accommodate this is a recidivist, which means you wouldn't even qualify for parole.*

*What I'm trying to make sure you understand is the severity of what your charges are and what the punishment could be, and you may be perfectly innocent of this and you're standing here before me presumed innocent; and I want you to know that...that I'm seeing it that way. But I also would hate to see you make a terrible* mistake by assuming that if you're convicted that the treatment would be light on this matter.

I take into consideration any offers that are presented to me as to an agreement – a plea agreement before we get to trial. But when we get to trial, it's going to be too late. And at that point, we'll have a trial; and if you're convicted, then, without benefit of an agreement between your counsel and the State, I will be deciding the sentence.

So I just wanted to have that discussion with you. Are there any questions you have of me?

MS. KELLY: No, sir.

THE COURT: Okay. Thank you.

Afterward, a large tall deputy escorted me back to the holding cell. Something happened to me that day that I can only describe as "an awakening." Of all the judges I've faced in various cities, counties, and states, the judge's remark about my record being sixty-two pages long struck a chord in me that broke a stronghold within me like broken glass on hot concrete pavement.

It's hard to describe if you weren't there that day in the courtroom to hear Judge Ballard speak. I heard compassion in his voice as he explained everything to me in such a heartfelt manner. I sensed the Judge cared and saw the wasted life I'd lived wanting better for me. I felt his speech was a God thing, and I knew after this sentence, I'd never be the same again.

Peace like a river flooded me within, and I was somehow liberated. Yes, I faced the judge once more about half an hour later and was sentenced to prison, but even so, I was still free!

If I had a white flag, I would have waived it in surrender. At this phase of my life, God met me and encouraged and strengthened me to go forward. Sixty-two pages later, this devotional was birthed and is given to you with the hope you would receive the gift of freedom and total release only God can and will provide through prayer.

This devotional is the fruit of the times I've read God's Word and prayed to Him myself. I have learned that He is my friend, sister, brother, parent, and constant companion. He is seen from Genesis to Revelation. From beginning to end, He is God. This devotional is 52 weeks long. It doesn't matter what time of year you pick this devotional up, there is no better time to start than now.

Following each week's devotion, there are four areas provided for you to personally journal. The first part allows you to reflect on the scripture given, a phrase in the prayer, or a word God has put in your spirit. Space is also provided for you to write out your own prayers. Then, as you go through each week, think about ways God reveals Himself to you and journal those encounters. And last, because God is for us, there is a fourth area for you to jot down names of loved ones or even strangers to take to the throne of mercy through the vehicle of prayer.

You may not be in a physical prison, but something has been or will tug on you and cause you to be tied up and bound. I assure you regardless of what or who it is, you can find freedom like me.

Sinful choices led me to this place with razor-wired fences; however, while I may still be bound through incarceration, yet I AM FREE!

If God can use such a sordid vessel as me, I KNOW He can make you fit for His service....LET'S BEGIN.

## Week 1

*In the beginning God created the heavens and the earth.*
Genesis 1:1

In the beginning GOD....I start this day with gratitude to the highest. You my Lord always was and always will be. There has never been nor ever will be a time when You have been nonexistent. All that occurs on this earthly plane I travel is known by You. Nothing catches You by surprise. There has never been a "time out" with You.

Why this knowledge doesn't sustain me in daily trials and difficulties, I am so unaware, Lord. If You took nothing and made everything I see, why do I find myself worrying, doubting, and fearing so often? I call out to You in all Your sovereignty to help me change my perspective today. I cannot explain creation; it just is. So help me to increase my faith in Your Word.

You designed everything in complete order. I seek You to destroy the chaos in my life that seeks to reign in my emotions and my mind. Help me to walk in the peace and love You've offered from the beginning. It has never been Your will for me to be one of little faith. I am to be a part of You and basking in Your love.

Help me call to mind that You not only created things but also You created us humans. Your fire of love has been blazing from the start. My earnest desire is to receive the love You give and return it to You and others. From the beginning, You are God. There is no end to You. From the darkness, the void, You created! I vow today to seek You wholeheartedly.

Because You are and always will be, I choose to rest in You. Whatever is within me that's not part of Your original design; I relinquish it to You. All I desperately want to be or do is what You've planned for me. I was on Your mind in the beginning. Take Your rightful place within me. You are God, and that's enough. Amen.

## ❧Reflections❧

## ❧Personal Prayer❧

## This Week I've Seen God

## People To Pray For

## Week 2

*Then the man said, "Your name will no longer be Jacob, but Israel, because you have struggled with God and with humans and have overcome."*
Genesis 32:28 (NIV)

Oh Father, how I glean hope from Your very Word. I have a chance against the powers of hell that at one time held me hostage. I've struggled within myself, with others and even with You, and You met me on my troubled road. How easy it is for me to relate with my forefather Jacob: a supplanter, a deceiver, and a manipulator. All these I've been in one form or another. For years I've tried to hold the reins and control my destiny, but You never gave up on me.

I've struggled. I've fought against You, myself, and loved ones; however, in You, I have prevailed. I thank You for the power of Your precious Holy Spirit. You have filled me with awe in changing my character and my desires.

You alone saved me from a lifetime of brokenness.

   I thank You for rescuing me. You offer me a place I can always run to. I look at the cross and see an invitation to come to You with Your outstretched arms. I find healing in every drop of blood You poured out for me on Calvary. In You, I have the assurance to run this race. I have reason to go on.

   In You, I find beautiful patient grace. Your Word draws me into a love that surpasses anything I've ever known. I couldn't go so far that You couldn't reach me. The depths of my sins, fears, and doubts weren't too deep You couldn't bring me out.

   The fight is over. I can finally live. You have taken me over barriers I could never have crossed without You. I thank You for Your peace and the satisfaction given by being in unity with you. You fill me like no other. I welcome You today; forever, I walk in your victory. You did what I could never do: You changed me. Amen.

## ❧Reflections❧

## ❧Personal Prayer❧

## ❧This Week I've Seen God❧

_____
_____
_____
_____
_____
_____
_____
_____
_____
_____
_____
_____

## ❧People To Pray For❧

_____
_____
_____
_____
_____
_____
_____
_____
_____
_____
_____
_____
_____
_____

## Week 3

*You intended to harm me, but God intended it for good to accomplish what is now being done, the saving of many lives.*
Genesis 50:20 (NIV)

Holy God, are You saying that You can take the ugliness in my life and create beauty from it? And, my hurts can be used to help others heal? You can turn my darkness into light? I am beyond amazed; Your grace is truly sufficient.

With You being God, there is room for a genuine turnaround in my life. Your magnificent glory has met my gory guilt and shame and empowered me. I can point out the evil that has been done to me; how be it that the light of Your Word shows me evil I've done to others as well. Your love is powerful and cleanses on both fronts. It is truly a double-edged sword. You fight on my behalf, and You strip me of all the dross that separates us.

There's been purpose in all of it. You have freed me to love and follow the path You showed me. You have restored me from a vessel of dishonor to a vessel of honor.

You've overruled the works of the enemies of my life to bring about Your desire. My heart is open to You. Fill me more and more with the strength to carry on. Show me the path You've chosen and help me to follow in pure obedience.

Use me for Your glory to point others to You. Use me as a catalyst to catapult the blind and broken to You. There is no purpose greater than showing You to a weary soul. Help me, Father, to lead the wanderer to the melodious song of salvation, to the heart of hope – from ashes of pain to the beauty of wholeness.

I thank You for removing the dust of destructive habits and replacing it with the pristine shine of peace and purpose. Your eternal presence has kept me, and I'll forever glory in it. HALLELUJAH! Amen.

## ❧Reflections❦

_____
_____
_____
_____
_____
_____
_____
_____
_____
_____
_____

## ❧Personal Prayer❦

_____
_____
_____
_____
_____
_____
_____
_____
_____
_____
_____

## ~This Week I've Seen God~

## ~People To Pray For~

## Week 4

*The Lord will fight for you; you need only to be still.*
Exodus 14:14 (NIV)

    Spirit of the living God, why is it so hard at times for me to trust You and be still? The voices from within challenge the truth. I know Your word is truth. Although You have never lost in war, I find myself walking in fear. Help me look above my circumstances to Your wonderful face. I need You to bring my memory back to past victories. Show me that You never change. What You did in yesteryear you're able to do even now.

    Help me respond to the truths You've displayed to me in the Bible, Your manual. I want to always know You as Savior, Deliverer, and Healer, my personal God. No one can avenge my enemies like You. You are the undisputed victor. Make my fears dissipate in the light of Your love. Open my eyes and let my focus remain on You. Continually show me Your heart. Help me stay confident in who You are. My aid comes from You. Not once have You failed me or cowered before anything that has risen in my life.

When the scars of life leave me weak, help me rest in Your strength. The power, love, and sound mind of Yours belong to me. I need your abundant assistance to receive it no matter what comes. Set my feet on the solid rock of truth, and I will stand still. If I truly learn these battles aren't mine, I can surrender all unbelief.

Your blood has made me an overcomer. You rose in order to make me a conqueror. As You fight, I'll stand still on Your promises that are yes and amen. So be it is Your solution to my problems. In obedience to Your word, I walk in faith.

Nothing that comes against me can win as I look to you. You are my glorious defender, so I choose to rest this week. Amen.

## ~Reflections~

## ~Personal Prayer~

## ❧This Week I've Seen God❧

## ❧People To Pray For❧

## Week 5

*God spoke to Moses: "Speak to the people of Israel. Tell them, I am God, your God. Don't live like the people of Egypt where you used to live, and don't live like the people of Canaan where I'm bringing you. Don't do what they do. Obey my laws and live by my decrees. I am your God.*
Leviticus 18:1-4 (The Message)

Eternal Father, in these verses, my eyes are open to Your love. I see that I am special to You. It's not Your will for me to follow the lead of any other. Your presence carries me. Any other things in the land that seek Your rightful place are pure idolatry. I want to be fully devoted to You.

You know the folly of following another. Lord, You know I've done so in my past; however, I have encountered You, my Defender, my Rescuer, and to go back will be to my demise.

You are My God. I no longer take Your love or Your amazing grace for granted. I seek You so I may taste real life. All my past idolatry only leads to emptiness – pure futility.

I am grateful that You are not a harsh Pharaohic taskmaster. Your commands are not to harm me, but to prosper me, to edify Me. Your heart rejoices to bless me. Help me not to live like the world, but as one who pleases You. I do not want to continually grieve Your Spirit.

Remind me that obedience to You will help me approach You more confidently. Deliverance from my selfish ways is my prayer. I ask Your help to live. Life is only found in You.

Thank you for Your whispers of sweet love to me. In my nakedness You show me my sinfulness and cover Me in Your righteousness. You flood my dark life with Your cloak of light, and I will forever seek You. I am Yours. You are mine. Amen.

## ✿Reflections✿

## ✿Personal Prayer✿

## ❧This Week I've Seen God❧

## ❧People To Pray For❧

## Week 6

*And there we saw the giants, the sons of Anak, which come of the giants: and we were in our own sight as grasshoppers, and so we were in their sight.*
Numbers 13:33

To the God who is ever-present and goes to battle for me, open my eyes to see who You've said I am. These giants seem to overwhelm and defeat me over and over again. Inwardly the battle is raging, and I feel so tired, so weary.

Help me take You at Your Word. I see weakness; You give strength. I see failure; You give success. My voice cannot make a sound; You put praise in my mouth. In my weariness, you give me perfect rest. Help me stop succumbing to the giants that seek to slay me.

Unless I receive virtue from You, I walk as one that's blind. I am unable to see the wondrous beauty of Your Word manifest in my life. I want to have experiential knowledge of

Your goodness. Cause Your truths to be accepted within me.

You say I am a peculiar child, a royal one. I want to believe it. I want Your Word to remove the falsehoods of my enemies. Yes, I am fighting the lies of the great liar Satan; but at times, I fight my own self. Victory is what You offer, and I desire the ability to walk in it. I hear You call to me from the piles of rubbish I've settled in. My need is for You to help me answer and be in agreement with You.

Turn my unbelief to belief. Help me break through the fog and walk in Your hope, Your radiant light. I vow this day to hold on to You knowing that the giants can't conquer us. Together we are one - I in You and You in me. Come what may, I trust the Holy Spirit to remind me of Your call to faith, to keep me seeing the Son and receiving His resurrection power. No giant can prevail as I look to You. Thanks to You, I am a giant slayer. Amen.

## ❧Reflections❧

## ❧Personal Prayer❧

## ᕿThis Week I've Seen Godᕿ

_____
_____
_____
_____
_____
_____
_____
_____
_____
_____

## ᕿPeople To Pray Forᕿ

_____
_____
_____
_____
_____
_____
_____
_____
_____
_____
_____
_____
_____
_____

## Week 7

*Only be careful, and watch yourselves closely so that you do not forget the things your eyes have seen or let them fade from your heart as long as you live.*
Deuteronomy 4:9a (NIV)

Oh, faithful God, how easy it is for me to look at the Israelites and wonder how they could forget all the things You showed them. Forgive me for forgetting all the deliverance and provisions You have so graciously shown me. I let Your faithfulness fade from my own heart and allow worry to crowd You out. Here I am surrendering all that I am. As I look to Your Word and my own life, You never leave me. You are always present. You are God alone.

I bow in humility and can barely look up because the shame of forgetting is so deep; however, Your righteousness covers me, and that's the only way I can look up. My food, clothes, and shelter You generously provide. The stoniness in my heart You've removed. You've calmed storms that have risen in my life. You so powerfully reached down in my pits of destruction and raised me up and out.

I trust You, my Redeemer. You are holy and so loving. My creator, take Your rightful place as Lord of all my affairs. I stand as a student before the teacher. I'm at Your disposal. You empower me to go forward. I love You and desire to never forget all of Your goodness to me. There is no other like You, and I will forever praise You.

My mind is filled with endless thoughts of your great acts. My heart bubbles with praise at Your mercy and forgiveness. You are the reason I can move on. Your presence in my life is miraculous. You'll never fade from this heart. I am sold out to You, and regardless of the clouds, I'll forever see You - the Lover of My Soul Jesus. Amen.

## Reflections

## Personal Prayer

## ❧This Week I've Seen God❧

## ❧People To Pray For❧

## Week 8

*Keep this Book of the Law always on your lips; meditate on it day and night, so that you may be careful to do everything written in it. Then you will be prosperous and successful.*
Joshua 1:8 (NIV)

Precious and powerful God, all You desire is for me to be victorious. With Your desire, You've left me with Your Word to prevail. Never have You given a command without the Holy Spirit's enabling grace. True prosperity and success come through You, the Everlasting Word.

Father, help me to fan the flame and hunger, and thirst after Your Word. There are times I get weary and allow my feelings to cause me to run from Your Word. Redirect my very being to come to You. Keep me running towards You and not away. Remind me of Your promises that never change. Close my ears from all the voices of this world that seek Your place.

Cause Your Word to lead me into all truth. Help me courageously live and proclaim Your Word as the General of Eternal Success.

Your Word frees me and puts me at oneness with You. The freedom You have given from the chains of death I fully receive today. Grace is so amazing and wonderful. You and the Word are One, and You are for us.

Cause me to meditate on every word You have spoken, whether command, promise, or direction; it is all for my good. From before the foundation of this world, You had me in heart and mind.

I glorify You, my Master, and my Love. Your mercies carry me on the wings of the Word. The greatest success I can ever accomplish is to be one with You for eternity. To see Your face and feel Your embrace will bring me joy beyond measure. To hear You call me your faithful servant will prosper my heart like no other.

I will meditate on Your Word and obey it until we meet. When I fall short, I will rely on the power of the Holy Spirit to prosper me in the arms that will never fail me. Amen.

## ～Reflections～

## ～Personal Prayer～

## ❧This Week I've Seen God❧

## ❧People To Pray For❧

## Week 9

### *Then Samson prayed to the Lord, "Sovereign Lord, remember me..."*
### Judges 16:28a (NIV)

Most Omnipotent God, I pray with a heart of gratitude for You knowing and always remembering me. You have a spot in Your heart just for me. I await the unfolding of today's events, for I trust Your all-seeing eye no matter what comes.

Help me remember You in all my endeavors. Help me hold on to Your precious promises that never fail. Remind me I am Yours and that I do have purpose. I am a chosen child of Yours. You are the Light that will never flicker out. Shine through me to others. I know that I am a vessel bought, saved and sanctified through the blood of Christ.

I thank You I will not have to carry the heavy load alone. Separation from You isn't possible. I appreciate Your heart for me. My rest in You allows me to walk undisturbed. You are my place of refuge. You never forget me. My prayers and songs of praise are sweet sounds to Your Holy ears. You've helped me overcome struggles that I never knew I could defeat. Victory is mine only in You.

I awake with joy and an open heart because I am known by You. Nothing I've done makes You run away from me. Your pursuit of me gives me reasons to continue the race of life. You never forget the characters in this story, and so many times, you rewrite the script.

I ask You to remember me, but more than anything to help me remember You. As gracious as You are to me, help me to be the same to others. Help me comfort my sisters and brothers with the same comfort You bestow upon me. Help me answer Your call to love You and my fellow man. Thank You for never forgetting nor leaving me on this journey forevermore. Amen.

## ❧Reflections❦

## ❧Personal Prayer❦

## ❧This Week I've Seen God❧

_____
_____
_____
_____
_____
_____
_____
_____
_____
_____

## ❧People To Pray For❧

_____
_____
_____
_____
_____
_____
_____
_____
_____
_____
_____
_____
_____

## Week 10

*The woman said to Naomi: "Praise be to the Lord, who this day has not left you without a guardian-redeemer"...*

Ruth 4:14a (NIV)

Your Word shall forever stand. You have never left me alone. A true Kinsman Redeemer You are. When I was enslaved in sin and fought against all You stood for, You purchased me anyway. You didn't buy me from one form of slavery to make me another type of slave. You made me an heir of Your glory. I became part of the Royal family.

You took my guilt and made me innocent. Your love freed and forgave me. Your hand reached out to me to come to You, and I won't release it. Where I was surrounded by dangers seen and unseen, You covered me and kept me safe. I do not need to walk in fear or dread. You give me more than I will ever deserve.

You are all that I need. I give up and take my place in the family. The past is gone, and I look into Your eyes at this moment. My future is in Your hands, and I praise You from now to eternity. I am redeemed by my Savior. I am washed and made new today. My wrongs are gone, and I can be who You intended.

You are my Guardian. Nothing I encounter is too much for You to handle. When I couldn't see the finish line in sight, You gently prodded me on. Your mercy holds me up and heals my brokenness. I have no reason to give up. My face beams with joy, because You are here with me.

Fear be gone. Shadows of darkness, I command you to flee in the name of my Kinsman Redeemer Jesus Christ. I release all sense of control and give it to You, Lord. Nobody can or will take care of me like You. No one is able but You. Thank you for my place in the family. I love You, Lord, Forever. Amen.

## ❧Reflections❧

## ❧Personal Prayer❧

## ❧This Week I've Seen God❧

_____
_____
_____
_____
_____
_____
_____
_____
_____
_____
_____
_____

## ❧People To Pray For❧

_____
_____
_____
_____
_____
_____
_____
_____
_____
_____
_____
_____
_____
_____
_____

## Week 11

*...Man does not see what the Lord sees, for man sees what is visible, but the Lord sees the heart.*
1 Samuel 16:7b (HCSB)

You are the all-seeing and all-knowing God, and I worship You. Who I am is who You say I am. My insufficiencies do not compare with Your great sufficiency within me. To look in the mirror of self, all I see is tattered and torn, but You say I am healed and whole.

Thank you for seeing me how You created me to be contrary to my actual actions. Cause Your heart to beat within my own. Let Your tenderness and compassion be revealed in me. Holy Spirit overcome my unloveliness with Your loveliness, my hard-heartedness with Your mercy. I give in to Your instructions, Your way.

Reach within me and draw out my real self that is pleasing to You. I acknowledge that there are times I go in opposition to Your truths for my own carnal reasoning, but my heart is after

You. Eternally I move as one that is not free, but the reality of my freedom is planted within the confines of my heart - the real one.

    Father, I desire to show Your transforming work in me in all I say and do. Cause what is in my heart to find a way to be outwardly displayed. You have always been my Helper, and I will forever turn to You. No matter where I go, I will cry out to You and wait on Your command to go right or left.

    You say I am holy and righteous because of Your holiness and righteousness, and I hold on to that. Your love and grace are enough to end my search for things that do not fulfill.

    I am grateful that Your eyes see and know the real me. Your hands hold my heart tightly and won't ever let me go. You walk with me on this journey and speak on my behalf daily, and I honor You forevermore. Amen.

## ❧Reflections❧

## ❧Personal Prayer❧

## This Week I've Seen God

## People To Pray For

## Week 12

*When all the people saw it, they fell facedown and said, "Yahweh, He is God! Yahweh, He is God!"*
1 Kings 18:39 (HCSB)

    You and You alone are God. Why do I often have to see Your hand before I easily accept Your sovereignty? You are God-always was-always will be. Your Lordship can never be usurped. I long to let go of my false sense of control in the circumstances that arise in my life.

    Who are You but God, the All-Sufficient One who meets all my needs? You are my Adonai adorned in perfect victory. There is no defeat in you. You, my God, are Jehovah Nissi, my own personal banner. You fight for me in battles that come forth, even those I bring on myself. Your strength is beyond any force that will come against me. You, Lord, fight against those who fight against me and contend valiantly for me.

    You are my God who has never abandoned me. You are always there for me. I need not doubt Your presence, which comforts me when the chaos and turmoil try to bring me down into a pool of confusion.

I bless Your name. You are God. I know You are God, the El Shaddai, the great Elohim, and Adonai. You are the awesome all-powerful. Nothing is lacking, nothing missing. You are my whole God, and because of You, I am one with You. Bless You. I praise Your name above all other names. In all that there is, You are.

I will stop running from You, and to Your arms, I come. To You, my God, I bring all my concerns and every supplication that weighs my heart down. There is no God like You. You are my Savior, Deliverer, Keeper, Giver of Peace, and Supplier of Needs, and You are more than words can ever express. Amen.

## ❧Reflections❧

## ❧Personal Prayer❧

## ~This Week I've Seen God~

_____
_____
_____
_____
_____
_____
_____
_____
_____
_____

## ~People To Pray For~

_____
_____
_____
_____
_____
_____
_____
_____
_____
_____
_____
_____
_____

## Week 13

*Then Elisha prayed, "Lord please open his eyes and let him see." So the Lord opened the servant's eyes.*
2 Kings 6:17a (HCSB)

I come not only to the All-Seeing God but to the Eye-Opening God. With a heart of gratitude, I come. When it seemed impossible for me to see my way, You called to me saying You are the way. In my brokenness, when it seems the pieces of my life are forever torn apart, You come and speak healing beyond what I've ever known. You, Lord, open my eyes during my darkest times and show me Your light, which helps me on my path.

I will continually seek You for Your eye-opening power. Worthy are You of all my prayers. You are my desire. Your love for me shows me the authenticity of Your sovereignty. You are such an awesome wonder. Blindness cannot last in Your presence- the Healer of Leprosy, Raiser of the Dead, Feeder of the Hungry, the Holiest of Holies.

Open my eyes that I see success instead of my failures. Help me see Your riches in place of my poverty. Open my eyes in faith and not the chains of fear. Your ability exceeds my inability.

Open my eyes to see the wondrous exchange I have with You. I have salvation instead of sins eternal loss, peace instead of chaos, trust instead of doubt and worry. You give me rest over weariness, love instead of hate, patience instead of impatience, strength instead of weakness, and more than I can recall.

You have given me a song in my heart where sadness had set up residence. Life took the place of eternal death. Continually open my eyes to see Your glory. You are visible to others in my life. My soul takes joy in seeing You in my daily affairs. Never can I thank you enough for giving me Your eyes in today's world. Forever I give You glorious praise. Amen.

## ❧Reflections❧

## ❧Personal Prayer❧

## This Week I've Seen God

_____
_____
_____
_____
_____
_____
_____
_____
_____
_____
_____

## People To Pray For

_____
_____
_____
_____
_____
_____
_____
_____
_____
_____
_____
_____
_____

## Week 14

*If my people, which are called by my name, shall humble themselves, and pray, and seek my face, and turn from their wicked ways; then will I hear from heaven, and will forgive their sin, and will heal their land.*
   2 Chronicles 7:14

O God, how You long for us to be in right relationship with You. You have a remedy to reconcile us even when we foolishly stray from You. In the darkest areas of sin, You so gently call us back. You want us to no longer be in captivity, and the door to prayer is our out.

When shame and brokenness seek to devour me, You call me to put down my shield of pride and wear the garment of humility. Lord, You know how difficult this is for me, but my true craving is for You. Any loss I've ever suffered isn't due to anything You've done, but You have so much You desire to give me. I want You to hear from me and most definitely need and seek

Your forgiveness. I may think I am strong and whole, but without You, I will never be whole.

I do acknowledge my need for the Holy Spirit's power to turn from my wicked ways and utterly forsake them. I cry out to You, and I depend on Your power to be who You've called me to be from before the foundation of the world.

I am Yours Lord. I am Your people. With You, I am redeemed. I am transformed by the power of Your love. I am one with You. I possess Your divine nature. Nothing can satisfy my hunger or quench my thirst as You. I will humble myself and pray and seek Your face for who You are. I want to desperately walk with You and before You as a pleasing one.

I trust in You, and Your power grants me the confidence to start over. As I obey Your commands, I give myself to You to become the whole, healed, and forgiven person that only You can make me be. Amen.

## ❧Reflections❧

## ❧Personal Prayer❧

## ❧This Week I've Seen God❧

## ❧People To Pray For❧

## Week 15

*And said, I beseech thee, O Lord God of heaven, the great and terrible God, that keepeth covenant and mercy for them that love Him and observe His commandments.*
Nehemiah 1:5

O Loving and Merciful God, when the ruins of my life seem to be forever done, I seek Your face. Your kindness keeps me rising from the error of my ways. I offer pure unadulterated thanks to You for not being done with me. I can't outdo Your love in my weakest moments. Your grace outlasts my most grievous failures. I am a living testimony of Your victorious mercy and grace that kiss and make me a true conqueror. I reign in the wings of Your love. Hallelujah!

Forever Your grace has been there to keep me from giving up. I rise because of Your awesome sacrifice – a display of love I can't properly define.

I bow in humility, asking for the power of the Holy Spirit to hold me up and succor me in being obedient to Your commands.

You are faithful to Your part of the covenant made between us. Help me to no longer be faithless and to love You wholeheartedly. Cause nothing else to have my heart's devotion. Release me from the sin of idolatry. You are to have Your rightful place in every part of my life.

Forgive me for the times I have disobeyed You and run towards my desires. Cleanse me from all my impurities and set me free. I know You became captive to death to bury the dominion of sin in my life. I am more than grateful that You rose with the keys to eternal life, opening the way for me to possess a real relationship.

I do beseech You day by day moment by moment, for there is no other god. I thank You that You are mine and I am Yours. Amen.

## ❧Reflections❧

## ❧Personal Prayer❧

## ❧This Week I've Seen God❧

## ❧People To Pray For❧

## Week 16

*Though He slay me, yet will I trust in Him: but I will maintain mine own ways before Him.*
*Job 13:15*

Father, regardless of my wounds and scars, I run into Your arms. I will forever press into Your generous care of me. No pain that comes can stop me from waiting on You to rescue me. Your deliverance has always been available.

To You, I come even when I do not understand the goings-on in my life. When my routine is interrupted, and I feel as though I carry the weight of the world on my shoulders, I still find freedom in coming to You.

I fall to my knees and experience Your redemptive power. Death can't hold me, whether it is the death of my dreams, goals or visions; I must maintain my trust in You. Never has failure or defeat been an attribute of Yours. Father, from where can I go that You are not there. I trust You. The shadows of this life seek to cover me and reign, but You burst through with Your abiding light. You make a path that liberates me from wilderness experiences. Your pursuit of me with such tender loving care encourages me to stand and not yield to my carnality.

You, Lord, are my Master, my Lord, my Salvation. I walk in Your resurrection power. You are my only hope. I will loudly roar my praises to You and only You. I submit to Your leadership. No suffering, trial, or tribulation will close my heart to Your victorious love. I press into You with all that I am and all that I am not.

My feet are marching forward to wherever You choose to lead me. Hold on to me as I aggressively cling to You. I can't let go. I won't let go. I have no desire to be away from You. I trust and love You always. Amen.

## Reflections

## Personal Prayer

## ❧This Week I've Seen God❧

## ❧People To Pray For❧

## Week 17

*Thou preparest a table before me in the presence of mine enemies: thou anointest my head with oil; my cup runneth over.*
*Psalm 23:5*

How grateful I am to the Shepherd of my soul. Your watchful eye over this sometimes wayward, dumb sheep has kept me from dangers seen and unseen. Your oil of protection has kept me in the driest seasons of my wanderings. You fill me when emptiness seeks to wear me out.

I am refreshed by Your cure. When I don't think I can make it any further and want to let go, You always revive me. When I foolishly desire to go towards the rapid streams of sin, those times You find me and reel me back in. When I want to wallow in shame and guilt, I look in Your face and see the twinkle in Your eyes that welcome me back in the fold. Your love is awe-inspiring.

You always prepare for me a grandiose feast. You are truly the Great Physician that nurses me back to wholeness. I don't deserve You, but You call me to oneness with You. There are so many pitfalls I walked into wide-eyed, and You still came to me and said, "Rise up My child!"

Of all that I've done, You still give me a place to honor and serve You. With You as my living hope, I know that I am not useless. You empower me to serve the entire body. I am forever indebted to You for Your goodness to me. I may be a battered, bruised and rebellious sheep, yet You beckon me home over and over again.

Thank You for carrying me, for making it possible for us to have a relationship. My every breath is because of You. I jump at Your command, and Your grip on me holds me near Your very heart. I lay down at Your feet and rest in You. I worship My Shepherd in all times. Amen.

## ❧Reflections❧

## ❧Personal Prayer❧

## ❧This Week I've Seen God❧

## ❧People To Pray For❧

## Week 18

> *O taste and see that the Lord is good: blessed is the man that trusteth in Him.*
> *Psalm 34:8*

Glorious God, I long to experience more of Your goodness and testify of it to the nations. Already I've come to know that purpose has been in any pain I've been through because I'm still here. I have recovered from the deep forks in the road that sought to take me under.

O the wonders of Your goodness to me. When the pit of hell welcomed me in my sinfulness, You rescued me and saved my poor wretched soul. I glorify You for all the times You stepped in and undid my foolish wiles. You've seen me through times when I was weary, and my knees were feeble. My weaknesses were no challenge for Your strength.

Lord, there have been times I cowered in a corner like an injured animal, and You pulled me out and into Your warm loving embrace. In Your hand, I am safe and secure.

When I ran after worthless endeavors with no good end in sight. Your indescribable love showed me a better way. There's never a moment I can ever say I was alone. You are always there just as You promised in Your Word. My love for You may not be perfected, but it will never come to an end. Your love for me has eased my distresses on more occasions than I can count.

I do trust You, and I accept the blessings of living a faith-filled life. You have never failed me. Your grace and favor are exceptional and most definitely undeserved. I can't say that my faith and obedience to Your Word are always unwavering, but Your character is always the same. I lean on Your integrity. Never have my needs been unmet. I am one with You, and that makes me walk in Your righteousness. I declare by faith that I am blessed because I do trust in You. Amen.

## ℘Reflections℘

_____
_____
_____
_____
_____
_____
_____
_____
_____
_____

## ℘Personal Prayer℘

_____
_____
_____
_____
_____
_____
_____
_____
_____
_____
_____
_____

## ❧This Week I've Seen God❧

## ❧People To Pray For❧

## Week 19

*With my whole heart have I sought thee: O let me not wander from thy commandments.*
Psalm 119:10

O Shepherd of my soul, lead, guide, and direct me. When my desire is to lean to my own sense of direction and I wander from Your path, please pull me back in. Draw me into the fold. You are the reason I move and have my very being. There are days I feel like I know the way on my own, but I know the deceiver of my heart is lying to me, fooling me.

Sometimes my actions prove that I either forget how great You are, or I take You for granted. I need You, and I yearn for You. With all my flaws and faults, I long to be the sheep that stays close to You. Your voice alone do I desire to hear and follow. I am ready Lord to yield to You.

No longer do I want to be caught up in searching in the wilderness of my own making. No longer do I desire to half-heartedly seek You, looking for You only to hear my SOS pleas. I want to give You all of my being. Cause the fire of Your divine will to burn within me. Perfect Your will in all my decisions and attitudes.

I seek to move according to Your plan. I will do what You do and speak what You speak. Empower me not to step aside from Your lead. No longer do I need to fear evil for in Your faithfulness You've never forsaken me.

With all my desire, I yearn for You and the rest I can only experience in You. Keep me from running toward things that will only leave me broken and in distress. I rejoice in Your love that always gives me another chance. Your words are only to bless me and give me life. Help me stop wandering and remain steadfast in You forever. Amen.

## ❧Reflections❦

## ❧Personal Prayer❦

## ❧This Week I've Seen God❧

## ❧People To Pray For❧

## Week 20

*Let not mercy and truth forsake thee: bind them about thy neck; write them upon the table of thine heart.*
Proverbs 3:3

    Kind and Ever Merciful God, help Your child not to forsake the virtues that are pleasing in Your sight. Give me the power, strength, and will to walk in Your ways. I welcome the death to self. Close the door of my heart that entertains hatred and all impurities. I worshipfully come to You for grace to turn from all that is evil.

    Draw out every form of hypocrisy that seeks to rule my every action. I acknowledge that there are times I operate in falsehoods. My desire is for verity to reign. Through every season of life help me to abhor and totally loathe things that are undesirable in Your eyes. You've given me Your Word to make me whole and in oneness with You.

I want to keep your Word in my eyes, heart, and forever displayed in my will. Where would I be without You and Your gracious love? My security in You keeps me from my waywardness.

The more I keep You close to me, the more I find it easier to strip myself of my unregenerate self. The change Your Word births in me makes my life practices renewed.

Adorn me in the holy attire that comes from only You. In You, I find wisdom, discernment, and the bond of wholeness. Remove the stones of discontent and disobedience from my heart. Clothe me in true and willing submission in mind, body, and spirit as You modeled in Your time here on earth. Cause me not to consider Your commands to be burdensome. Never have You given a Word to be a hardship to me or to be troublesome to me. I carry Your Word in my heart to live and share with the nations that they may come to know You, to love you. Amen.

## ❧Reflections❧

## ❧Personal Prayer❧

## ❧This Week I've Seen God❧

## ❧People To Pray For❧

## Week 21

*A man's heart deviseth his ways: but the Lord directeth his steps.*
Proverbs 16:9

God of purpose and director of my steps, order my ways in the way in which You'd have me go. Straighten the crooked paths and keep me on the straight and narrow. I do not know how to make my way sure. I need You, Father. Purge the dross of sin and selfishness that is deep within my nature.

Your Word clearly states that the heart of man is wicked above all; I cannot trust my own. I cause pain in my life and the lives of others. My intent is not to depart from Your guidance, but at times I go against what I know is true. Search my innermost being and shine Your light of love, grace, and mercy on the dust of my misdeed, untruths, and deceptions. Make me holy and cause me to be Your good and faithful child. I want to live in a way that You will delight in me. Establish, perfect, strengthen, and settle me. Grasp onto me, and as I cling to You Lord, never let me go. Keep me close to Your heart. Cause our hearts to beat as one.

 I seek You to correct me, to instruct and direct me for I know You truly have my best interest at heart. I am wanted by You, and I am grateful. When I fail and falter, You pick me up and restore me. You heal what is broken and bind what's wounded. I trust You and choose to glorify You. You are my Portion, my Refuge from the storm even though I create them at times. In Your wrath, You'd bring me to nothing, but in Your love, You bring me up. I know that Your perspective causes me to rise and stay on the track that You've made for me. I love You. Amen.

## ❧Reflections❧

## ❧Personal Prayer❧

## ❧This Week I've Seen God❧

## ❧People To Pray For❧

## Week 22

*Behold, God is my salvation; I will trust, and not be afraid: for the Lord JEHOVAH is my strength and my song; He also is become my salvation.*
Isaiah 12:2

From You, my Savior come ALL the answers to my entreaties. You are my strength, salvation, and song. I am empowered to go on just at the whisper of Your precious yet powerful name. In You, Jehovah, is my victory, banner, righteousness, sanctification, and my all in all.

Trusting You becomes easier as I take You at Your Word. There is no lack in You. I rest in Your deliverance. Forever will I praise You and tell of Your wondrous deeds. I am able to experience liberty because You did all that was necessary for it to be my reality. No other but you will I serve and remain faithful to. Even in those times I falter, I take joy in Your mercy. I run to You, where I can obtain the cleansing power of Your gracious love.

When my emotions try to get the best of me and weigh me down in defeat, I am grateful to the Holy Spirit's reminder that my hope is in You. The cry of truth resounds in my heart, and I am encouraged to receive the strength found in You. I am comforted and reminded to walk as the resurrected one You made me to be.

Weakness and feelings of despair must fade in Your presence. I am able to obtain the dreams and goals that You've placed within my heart. My visions are able to become reality.

My greatest desire is to be in union with You, my Jehovah. I don't possess a need You can't meet. As the Alpha and Omega, You give me the strength to start over. Your healing virtues put me back together again when I'm falling apart. I exalt You because You are my God, and no other can take Your place. I love you.

## ☙Reflections☙

## ☙Personal Prayer☙

## ꙳This Week I've Seen God꙳

## ꙳People To Pray For꙳

## Week 23

*When thou passest through the waters, I will be with thee; and through the rivers, they shall not overflow thee: when thou walkest through the fire, thou shalt not be burned; neither shall the flame kindle upon thee.*
Isaiah 43:2

    I am grateful for You, my Hope of Glory, and the power You impart within me to withstand hardships. You never promised me a life of no trials or tribulations, but You did promise me Your presence. You have assured me that forever You'd be with me. Oh, the gratitude my heart experiences today for You are the Ever Presence that protects and defends me.

    Sometimes the current of waters seek to knock me off balance, and Your right hand upholds me. You do not allow me to remain in a state of defeat. My eyes see the turmoil that is coming to overwhelm me, but being the Father that You are, You instruct me to look in Your face, hold Your hands, and follow You to the shores of safety. My help comes from You. I am secure in You. The rivers seem to be an instrument of death designed to sweep over me and take my breath away. At times I think I'm going under never to return, and You lift me way above the waves. Father, I thank You for holding me in the curve of Your arms. Your shoulders have become a place of comfort. It is in Your strength that I find the resolve to go on – to live! I love You, Lord.

The fires of difficulty come to devour me. As I read and trust Your Word, I am confident that I will come out unburned without even the smell of smoke. You're not a God of partiality, so I look at how You kept Daniel and the Hebrews through a night in the fiery furnace, and I praise You in advance for my deliverance. I surrender to Your Lordship. You are able, and because You are a Consuming Fire, any challenge that comes my way won't overtake me. I welcome and continuously invite You to stay with me and ask You to help me stay with You. Amen.

## ❧Reflections❦

## ❧Personal Prayer❦

## ❧This Week I've Seen God❧

## ❧People To Pray For❧

## Week 24

*No one is like You Lord; You are great, and Your name is mighty in power.*
*Jeremiah 10:6 (NIV)*

Gracious God whose name is above every name, I come to You in gladness and exceeding joy. To the ends of the earth, I will forever offer praise to You, the God of Gods, King of Kings. You don't just do right all the time; You are Righteousness.

At your name, every knee will bow. This, Lord, is not just physical knees, but knees of rebellion, disobedience, sicknesses, and everything unlovely. You are the ultimate power, and there is no other but You. For the times I display behavior as if I am my own god, remind me of truth. Remind me that Your sovereignty can't be fully comprehended, but I must submit to it. I need You to repeatedly remind me that my ways are never higher than Yours. You alone can and will help me. Before I send up a plea for Your aid, You already know it.

Your name is most awesome and more glorious than I can imagine. For any ailments that come to my vessel of clay, You prove to be Jehovah-Rapha. When I am going astray and wandering like a nomad, You pull me in as my Jehovah-Rohi – the Lord, my Healer. No one can contend for me as You my Jehovah-Nissi; You are the Lord my Banner. When the enemy comes in like a flood, You set up a standard in my behalf. As my provider of natural or spiritual deficiencies, You continue to be Jehovah-Jireh, the Lord my Provider.

Your name is not lacking in any area of my life; You've become my very life. In You, I find comfort, grace, peace, love, faith, redemption, salvation, a hiding place and so much more.

I bless Your name with all that is within me. I seek all that You are and ask You to take me even in my feebleness. You and no one else are exalted. Hallelujah. Amen.

## Reflections

## Personal Prayer

## ☙ This Week I've Seen God ☙

## ☙ People To Pray For ☙

## Week 25

*The Lord is good to those whose hope is in Him, to the one who seeks Him.*
Lamentations 3:25 (NIV)

 Dear Heavenly Father, I've known Your goodness in time of peace and even in troublesome days. Thanksgiving swells within me for how You have shown up in every circumstance that has arisen in my bright days or gloomy nights.

 Your compassion keeps me like a traveler on a hot desert land, always seeking You. You are worthy.

 Because of your holiness, my hope has no room for despair, depression, or disappointment to reign. It is You who has brought me out of the miry clay and every pit of destruction. The enemy and his tactics have never been able to prevail.

My heart longs to follow You and serve You all my days. There is no real satisfaction anywhere that You are not present. I seek You and all that You call righteous and pleasing.

I give up my life and its emptiness to be unified with You. The world has nothing of lasting value for me. I look to You and Your beauty and find myself rising to the newness of days basking in Your love.

I know You are the only true and wise God, and to You, I yield my will. Help me share the hope you give me with those that cross my path. Open my eyes to see who I can share You with. Prepare hearts. Encourage me not to be a coward or one that walks in fear when it comes to telling others where hope lies – in You.

When the heap of ashes in my life causes me to want to give up, I look to You and find the oil of joy and a crown of inexpressible beauty. You bring words from scripture that tell me, "It's not over." I love when You say, "Just rest in My plan, rest my child." Thank you, Lord, for taking delight in me and never giving up on me. In Jesus' name, Amen.

## Reflections

## Personal Prayer

## ❧ This Week I've Seen God ❧

## ❧ People To Pray For ❧

## Week 26

*Therefore say unto the house of Israel, Thus saith the Lord God; Repent, and turn yourselves from your idols; and turn away your faces from all Your abominations.*
Ezekiel 14:6

My Most Merciful God, I am amazed at Your unfailing love. You cry out to me to come back to You and leave behind my mirthless idols. How many times have I either tried to be my own god or made one out of other things and people? I've broken Your heart more times than I care to admit.

Your Word calls me to turn my face from my abominations, but Lord where can I go? I am thankful You call me to Yourself. Help me to die to my foolish self-will. I submit to You wholeheartedly. I undress from my shame and regret and walk in the redemption You give me.

In You I am full, whereas the idols never satiated me. I turn to You to shake off my chains of sin. My heart longs for the relationship with You that restores my faith in Your enduring mercy. No more depending on untrustworthy idols. I am most grateful that even though I turned from You, Your desire for a broken vessel as me is still there. You, the Anchor of my Soul, have never left me shipwrecked.

You've opened my eyes to a heavenly perspective, and I don't ever desire to turn away from You. My hope and eternity are found in You. My soul is guarded by Your love.

You never gave up on me, and I repent and turn from all the influences of life that separate us. Your arms open wide to receive me even though I don't fully know why. You stay when all others either walk or fall away. Thank You that nothing separates me from Your love. The one constant in my life is You. I come back to You forever grateful. In Jesus' name, Amen.

## ❧Reflections❧

## ❧Personal Prayer❧

## ❧This Week I've Seen God❧

## ❧People To Pray For❧

## Week 27

*Then this Daniel was preferred above the presidents and princes, because an excellent spirit was in him.*
Daniel 6:3a

Lord of Hosts, thank You for the examples You give in Your Word of sisters and brothers of old that stood in faith before You. I seek Your spirit of excellence that was displayed in Daniel. I'm grateful that You've made it clear excellence isn't perfection as I know it, but it is wise behavior. Fill me with Your power to stand as one of courage in the face of my adversity.

God help me to be persistent in prayer. Cause me to trust You as my Protector. Do not allow the fear of other's opinions to cause me to back away from You. Grant me the boldness to speak Your Word before any audience.

As a child of God, remind me that I am of royalty. I am a preferred being loved by the King of King. Help me to bless Your name with my entire being. I will be one that praises You for all Your benefits. You always carry me, and I should never shrink from the battles of life. They are not mine anyway, and in Your hands, I experience outlandish victory.

You are the God I serve, the only true God, and Your deliverance is mine. No lion can prowl that You can't stop. If the stone in front of the cave you were entombed in was moved, why should I fear the stone of any raging enemy?

I decree and declare prosperity in my life. No hurt, harm, or powers can take me out. The sword of Your mouth cuts in shreds the enemies that come to take me down. There is no one like You God. Impart Your spirit of excellence in me. Cause me to be wise in all circumstances. Help me fully trust You. In Your exalted name, I pray. Amen.

## ❧Reflections❧

## ❧Personal Prayer❧

## ❧ This Week I've Seen God ❧

## ❧ People To Pray For ❧

## Week 28

*And I will give her her vineyards from thence, and the valley of Achor for a door of hope; and she shall sing there, as in the days of her youth, as in the day when she came up out of the land of Egypt.*
Hosea 2:15

Restorer of My Soul, You meet me in my bondage, lead me through the wilderness and bless me there; never do You leave me down. As I follow You, I rise. In my lewdness, You rescued me and covered me with Your righteousness. In my instability and grand acts of unfaithfulness, You gave me a reason to carry on.

In the desert of trouble that I traveled willfully, You showed me that a door of hope was available and open. I can expect Your Word to perform what You intend to be accomplished in my life. I lived a life of brokenness, and You brought healing to me. The judgment I deserved You withheld. The grace I didn't deserve You bountifully lavished upon me.

In pure rebellion, I followed the dictates of the world and my fleshy desire, and You rewarded me with steadfast love and tenderness.

As the children of Israel sang with joy for the glorious triumph you offered them, You've placed a song of praise in me. Your hand that wrought victory in the battles of my life is the same hand that embraced and comforted me. You are my holy habitation.

Forgive me for my waywardness in sinning against You. I caused so many unnecessary troubles, and as a last resort, I sought You. I was so blind I couldn't see You were waiting on me to be gracious to me. Lord, totally restore me and help me to obliterate all the things in my life that drew me so far from You. I will never experience love as You give. You're the very air I breathe. Cause Your divine fire to purify me. In Your matchless name, I pray. Amen.

## ❧Reflections❧

_____

## ❧Personal Prayer❧

_____

## This Week I've Seen God

## People To Pray For

## Week 29

*He will turn again, He will have compassion upon us; He will subdue our iniquities; and thou wilt cast all their sins into the depths of the sea.*
*Micah 7:19*

God of Abraham, Isaac, and Israel today, I recognize the great and complete forgiveness You so freely give. I cannot tell how far the east is from the west, but You remove my sins that far away from us. It is clearly evident You do not reward us for our iniquities as we deserve. When I allow the lusts of my flesh and my sensuality to reign, You mercifully forgive me. You take me back as if I've never sinned against You.

I pray that Your glory forever stands. You remain the same. Because of You, I am established before You. No one can snatch me out of Your hand. Again and again, You've displayed marvelous works in my life. My sins have been crimson red, and in compassion, You've made them as white as wool. The exchange You offer is unbelievable. You give holiness to a naturally unholy being. You draw me to You from the darkness and shine light in every crevice of sin. In all of my harlotry, You receive me as Your own bride.

You cover, protect, and provide for me like no other. You take the worst I have and give me Your best. Not once do You use my past evils against me. You love me as if I never walked away in an adulterous manner.

You've stood for me and never left me when I walked the crooked paths of death. Thank You for accepting and changing me. You said You come to seek and save the lost, and that was truly me. Your every promise is "Yes" and "Amen." I now live in Your life. I'm hidden in You, one with You. Forever will I cry out Hallelujah to You, the Holy of Holies. Praise You for the miraculous gift of forgiveness. In His name, Amen.

## ❧Reflections❧

## ❧Personal Prayer❧

## This Week I've Seen God

## People To Pray For

## Week 30

*The Lord is good, a stronghold in the day of trouble; and He knoweth them that trust in Him.*
Nahum 1:7

    Good and powerful God, upon You I lean forever as my strength in the weakest and darkest of times. Your presence is my comfort. You take me from glory to glory. All other ground is truly sinking sand. It is in Thee that I stand unshaken.

    The intimacy we share helps free me from the anxiety that troubles seek to bring into my life. I hear and know Your voice of deliverance. I will forever let my praises ring to You and of Your honor I can't help but tell all who will hear. My footsteps will only tread where you lead. Following any other is pure futility.

    You alone are good, and any goodness I have is wrapped in You. No fire is too hot for Your hand to save. You're acquainted with all of my ways, even when I get off path; yet You choose to still love me and show Your goodness. When in the scorching degrees of a wilderness of my own making, Your grace still shines forth and saves me.

There is no other god in all the universe. For those who don't come to know You, they only exist and don't experience the abundant life You give. All we need is in You. There's no power that can overtake You. All power is in and from You.

Thank You for being the One that never fails. There is no error in You. Awesome and great are You. No one or nothing can stand as You. Your mercy abounds at all times. Every time I inhale and exhale, I have reason to praise You. As Your most precious work, I am grateful for the perfection of my organs and the blood flow in my heart and veins. I live because You live, and I trust You. In Your name, Amen.

## ❧Reflections❧

## ❧Personal Prayer❧

## ❧This Week I've Seen God❧

## ❧People To Pray For❧

## Week 31

*Yet I will rejoice in the Lord, I will joy in the God of my salvation.*
Habakkuk 3:18

My saving God, my joy is found in You. In You Lord, I am joyful despite what comes my way. Family matters may be in a frenzy. Finances may be falling as each day goes by. Friends may misunderstand me and walk away, Yet I will rejoice in You. You are the Prince of Peace when chaos calls. When I feel like I can no longer hold on, Your hand lifts me up and stabilizes my soul.

I do not have to succumb to the terrifying fears that want to drive me in isolation. The enemy of my soul seeks to slaughter me, but You, God, step in and place me on solid ground. You're proven Yourself more times than I can count. Why do doubts assail me at times? You saw me as I was on the rapid slippery slope that leads to death. How lovingly You just picked me up and embraced me as the stray sheep I was.

My own foolishness never separated me from Your lasting love.

    I rejoice because I am assured that with You for me, no one can be valiant against me. Victory will always be mine, and I can claim with You that I am a conqueror; in fact, more than a conqueror. Because of You, I rejoice that my soul will not see the eternal damnation it rightfully deserves.

    As I walk in Your strength, I need not worry about the outcome of circumstances. In You, I can rest from the battles at hand. No giant can defy me because of Your presence. Mountains can block my way, but at Your Word, it must move, and I go over with a surpassing victory. You, the God of Possibilities, grant me courage amid seeming impossibilities. I rejoice in You Lord. Amen.

## ❧Reflections❧

## ❧Personal Prayer❧

## ❧This Week I've Seen God❧

## ❧People To Pray For❧

## Week 32

*And I will strengthen them in the Lord; and they shall walk up and down in His name, saith the Lord.*
Zechariah 10:12

Oh my, God of Israel, how Your Word shows me my Israelitish ways. Your grace and mercy have been extended to me as it was to them. Even though I, like them, forsook You and followed other gods, You still came to redeem me. You took Your garment of righteousness and covered me with it. In Your loving kindness, You sanctified me for service to You and even the world.

Where I lived a shallow life and lost the blessings You've imparted in my life, You return and give me increase. Not once did You close the door of your heart to me. Lord, You welcome me back with open arms and bring me out of the stormy weather. As You parted the Red Sea for the Israelites and destroyed their enemies, so You do for me. When I walk away and live as an orphan, you call me back to my place in the family. The consuming fire that You are burns the dross of sinfulness out of me and conquers these that so blatantly oppose me.

 My security is found in You. No longer must I travel as a wandering nomad. My place in You is sure. The seas of distress may wash over me, and the waves may make me a little shaky, but I do not go under. Your love causes my enemies to be confounded and ashamed.

 I have been walking with my head bowed in shame and regret, but You call me to a higher place. You tell me to look up and walk to You for liberation. Your smile gives me hope to carry on. You promise that I will walk up and down in Your name. Oh, the power in Your name! The power of you, God, strengthens me to move boldly in Your will. I will follow You to the ends of the earth. You, the Blesser of Outcasts, will forever have my praise. Amen.

## Reflections

## Personal Prayer

## This Week I've Seen God

## People To Pray For

## Week 33

*But unto you that fear my name shall the Sun of Righteousness arise with healing in His wings; and ye shall go forth, and grow up as calves of the stall.*
Malachi 4:2

Lord of Hosts, King of Kings, I eagerly await the day of Your return. All that is broken or wounded shall be made complete. Those who honor and totally revere Your name will be full of joy immeasurably. Shall I run and leap like calves released from their stalls? Shall I possess laughter that seems unending? Will I bow in humility and gratitude for Your graces and mercy upon my life?

Oh, Returning King, I do not know why You love me or how I will stand in the tangible presence of Your love. Father, I just want to see You. I want to embrace You and be held by You - the end of all pain and sorrow and the awful dominion of sin in my life. I await the day that all wickedness, my own and others, will be forever destroyed. Lord, how will I bask in eternal light, no more darkness.

The work You began in me will be complete at Your return. Jesus, I'm ready to be totally healed, to be able to walk in wholeness, and to be able to behold Your beautiful countenance. Oh, Lord, come quickly. Even so, Lord come. I anticipate days of continuous praise to You that no other deserves. The streets of gold may be impressive, even the pearly gates, but nothing will have me in awe like just seeing You.

I pray today that You prepare my heart to be forever knit together with You. Use me as a light on this earth to help others see and come to know You. Lord, my hands and feet are Yours to serve until You return. I cry out to You from the depths of my heart and say, "Come, Returning King." In Jesus' name, Amen.

## ❧Reflections❧

## ❧Personal Prayer❧

## ❧ This Week I've Seen God ❧

## ❧ People To Pray For ❧

## Week 34

*Blessed are the pure in heart: for they shall see God.*
Matthew 5:8

To You, my Lord, who creates hearts that are pure and clean, I come for help. I do not want a heart that is impure and divided, my Lord. I ask for the conviction of the Holy Spirit and His empowering strength to forsake my sins and the desire to return to them. I don't want anything to hinder me from seeing You.

As I draw near to You, according to Your Word, I'm confident You'll draw near to me.

I seek a heart that's truly after You. Build up Your character within me. Keep me near to Your heart and hold me close and tenderly. Shine Your love through every part of my heart and line my actions up with Your perfect will. Where bitterness, anger, or resentment seek to darken my heart, let your healing Word revive and restore me. Holy Spirit, You are my counselor, and I seek to be obedient to Your wisdom.

I ask that You fill my heart with love and compassion. Remove fear and confusion from within me and help me to be full of faith in You and walk in Your peace. Lead me in the ways of righteousness. Cause me to worship You in spirit and truth. Give me a heart surrendered to You, a heart that will live a sacrificial life.

Purify my heart. Let me rest in the hope that you are in every situation. Make me whole where I have travailed in brokenness and weariness.

I ask that I seek Your face more than any benefit You offer. As You gave of Yourself, help me do so as a follower of You. Transform my heart from its state of deadness and bondage. As I become purer and see You clearer, help me live according to Your good, acceptable, and perfect will. In Jesus' name, Amen.

## ~Reflections~

## ~Personal Prayer~

## ❧This Week I've Seen God❧

## ❧People To Pray For❧

## Week 35

*Jesus said until him, "If thou canst believe, all things are possible for him that believeth."*
Mark 9:23

Holy are You, the God that makes my seeming impossibilities bow and become possibilities. My fears do not come because of any frailties or weaknesses in You, but because of my own. There are times I fail to take You at Your Word and find myself sinking, even then You bring me up from the fall. Father, You'd think I'd learn from all my experiences in seeing You bring me up and out of my trials. Forgive me for my stout heartedness and rebelliousness.

I know that my desire is to have an undivided heart and trust wholly in Your Word. You told me trials would come, but I am to take courage and walk in Your prevailing power. In Your presence, what's dead must be resurrected. The crooked areas of my life must be straightened, the broken made whole, and the rough smoothed out.

Your word increases my faith, and I ask that You increase my hunger for Your Word. Cause my faith to be active with no room for doubt based on what I see. There's no way I can please You without real faith, and it comes from trusting Your word. You cannot, nor ever will fail or lie.

Oh God, I know that nothing is too difficult or challenging for You. Cause me to live my life according to this truth. In my impatience, help me to trust Your timing. Increase my faith that no calamitous mountain will send me running except into Your arms where I will be safe.

Lord, I do believe that You can do what no other can. The foundations of this world were made from nothing but Your Word. The sun, the rain, snow, and hail only exist because of You. What problem can arise in my life that's too big for You? Keep my eyes focused on You and Your marvelous glory. With You is no failure. I trust You Lord. Amen.

## ❧Reflections❧

_____
_____
_____
_____
_____
_____
_____
_____
_____

## ❧Personal Prayer❧

_____
_____
_____
_____
_____
_____
_____
_____
_____
_____

## ❧ This Week I've Seen God ❧

## ❧ People To Pray For ❧

## Week 36

*And when Jesus saw her, He called her to Him, and said unto her, Woman, thou art loosed from thine infirmity.*
Luke 13:12

Father, I don't always recognize the things that keep me bowed over, or may I honestly say I don't always confess them, but I know that only You can release me and straighten me out. In You is the answer to my every problem, a cure for every illness. See me, Father, and the shackles that bind me. Set me free. Your Word states that whom the Son sets free is free indeed. I seek this "indeed" freedom.

For years I've worried within and without. I surrender and give these battles to You that I may experience a lasting victory. I am tired of using crutches when in You is the healing that will allow me to leap over obstacles and be the conqueror You intended.

Lord, I am tired. I tire of trying to find my own remedies. I sought answers in places and people that You did not send me to. Your call to me has been ignored numerous times. Forgive me, Lord. I've had no success in lifting myself from the infirmities that ruled me for so long. I'm weak, weary and worn out from all the resources I've tried. The ashes and ruins of my efforts have overwhelmed me. Release me, Lord, from the things I've clung to that were of no value or use to me.

I'm tired of falling apart, but I hear You calling me to come to You. Yes, I'm bent over, crawling, unable to look up, but the closer I come, I am more able to breathe, to receive Your Spirit. I come to You open and honest because You already know. In my transparency, I say, "Take me and do with me as You will." Burn the dross out of me and help me to truly believe Your Word. You said I am loosed; I am released. Assist me with walking as a free delivered child of God. Your Word stands, and nothing can destroy the power that emanates from it. I fully receive it and will stand in its strength. To the emancipator, I come and will remain in Jesus' name, Amen.

## ❧Reflections❧

## ❧Personal Prayer❧

## ❧This Week I've Seen God❧

## ❧People To Pray For❧

## Week 37

*When Jesus saw him lie, and knew that he had been now a long time in that case, He saith unto him, Wilt thou be made whole?*
*John 5:6*

Jehovah-Rapha, the Lord my Healer, I do want to be made whole. I do not want to continue to walk in brokenness and with wounds seeping with sinfulness. The scars of my errors do not have to be signs of who I am, only where I've been and who I was. Be seen in me and heard in my voice of faith. I do not want to remain in desperation, but I'd love to journey on my course as one delivered.

Redeem me and use me as a vessel. You speak truthfully of Your redeeming power, love, and grace.

I want to be made whole, and no longer live in my past shame and guilt. No longer do I desire to fulfill the lusts of the flesh, but I want to walk in the fulfillment of Your purpose for my life. I want to be made clean. Breathe on me breath of God and transform me. I open up every part of my mind, will, and spirit and offer You full access. You restore all that I've messed up with poor choices and pure rebellion. For all of the turmoil and tribulations I've endured and even caused, You can and do use them for Your glory and my good as I submit to You.

I have agonizing longings that I can't put into words, and You give me Your Holy Spirit to pray for me. Release the potential within me that I was unaware that I possessed. The treasures, talents, and gifts that You gave me, cause me to utilize them.

Lord, I am Your child, and I do want to be made whole. Help me take my place in You. Lift up my head and point me in the right direction. I will follow You. I'll forever be grateful for the healing You do in my life. Forsake not the work of Your hands and help me. In Jesus' name, Amen.

## ❧Reflections❧

## ❧Personal Prayer❧

## ❧ This Week I've Seen God ❧

_____
_____
_____
_____
_____
_____
_____
_____
_____
_____

## ❧ People To Pray For ❧

_____
_____
_____
_____
_____
_____
_____
_____
_____
_____
_____
_____
_____
_____

## Week 38

*Rejoicing in hope; patient in tribulation; continuing instant in prayer; Distributing to the necessity of saints; given to hospitality.*
Romans 12:12-13

Holy God, help me to be one that's accountable to Your call for my life. Whatever my lot is, You expect me to step up to the plate, and I want to. Help me to grow in the knowledge of who You are and be one that follows You closely. Whether an apostle, pastor, teacher, or lay person, You've given me the command to pray without ceasing. You've called me to study Your Word and to go forth sharing Your goodness and truth.

Help me, Father, to be a builder of Your Kingdom. Place servants in my path that I can assist in their personal call and give me helpful, loving servants to do the same for me. Use us together to cause a dying world to connect with

You, the living Savior. Let us live in such a way that amazing things are accomplished everywhere we go that You may be glorified. Help us to be good stewards of all You provide that we continually give ourselves to You.

In humility, help us bow before You on bended knee trusting You will hear and answer our prayers. Assist and encourage other saints through us. Use us to lead lost sheep back into the flock following You, the True Shepherd. Give us knowledge of Your Word and assist us in effectively using it that blind eyes will be opened. As we continually pray and give ourselves to the ministry of the Word, remove the stoniness from the heart of the listeners that they will gladly submit to Your Lordship. We pray to You, the Only True God, who leaves us no room to doubt. We serve the True and Living God whose Word never fails. Your Word is not futile and is able to lift us over the winds of calamity. We give ourselves to You and all that You are. Take all of us and use us to draw the lost to You. In Jesus' matchless name, Amen.

## ❧Reflections❧

## ❧Personal Prayer❧

## This Week I've Seen God

## People To Pray For

## Week 39

*But we will give ourselves
continually to prayer, and to the
ministry of the Word.*
*Acts 6:4*

Master and Savior of the eternal Church, there are many in the body and much to be done. I ask You to help us devote ourselves to pray steadfastly and to the ministry of Your Word. Let us not be selfish in our prayers nor slow to serve each other. We desire strength not ever to become complacent or lack concern for the entire body.

Lord, cause us to minister not only in Word but more so in action and deed. Let not our daily actions defame You in any way. We seek Your light to shine through us and glorify You. In all that we do, help us abandon ourselves that You are clearly seen. As we keep coming to You, Lord, take selfishness from us and let submission to You be our top priority.

Help us be faithful to You and constantly displaying Your love. We need Your wisdom to be given to us as we bring our supplications to You.

It is not my desire to be hypocritical, walking in pretensions, but one that comes to You in transparency. I desire to do so with my sisters and brothers in this realm as well. Whatever adjustments I need to make in this life to serve You and Your people, show me and give me the power of Your Spirit to align myself with Your Word.

Father, as I pray to You and receive Your guidance and direction, help me to follow with no regard for applause or approval of man. I want to be in true communion with You. I know that this will endow me with the strength to persevere. Surely my obedience is the positive response that will bring joy to Your heart.

You know my desire to pray and serve this world with Your life-changing word so that we'll be with You in the new world to come. Thank You, Father, for making Yourself accessible to us. To You, I'll forever run. You are my safety net, and I'll forever follow you. Amen.

## ❧Reflections❧

_____
_____
_____
_____
_____
_____
_____
_____
_____
_____

## ❧Personal Prayer❧

_____
_____
_____
_____
_____
_____
_____
_____
_____
_____
_____

## This Week I've Seen God

## People To Pray For

## Week 40

*And He said unto me, "My grace is sufficient for thee; for my strength is made perfect in weakness.*
2 Corinthians 12:9a

Most gracious God, I thank You for the loving-kindness and mercy You offer to me when I feel overwhelmed with the affairs of this life. There are times I believe the weight of my troubles is more than I can bear. All I can see is pain and weakness. I see no way out. The waters are deep and full of darkness. I need relief, I'm sure, but I hear You saying Your grace and strength supersede what my senses are telling me.

All I can see is my scars, and I want instantaneous healing and the deliverance I know You're able to give. I find myself listening with my heart, and I'm ready to trust who You are because You suffered for me to be saved. I have to learn in the midst of these difficulties that You give me what I need to carry on victoriously. You in Your Sovereignty know what I need more than I think I know.

Speak to me, Lord, and help me to listen and lean on Your during these valley times. I've learned from Your Word that You've overcome the world so I can too in Your strength. Help me to release myself to You totally and not partially, not just in good times.

I want comfort, but I must trust You as You lay blocks of character in me. Although the mortar may be what I call challenges, You are sealing me. I go through these times with gratitude that Your presence is available to me, and the gift of peace is mine.

Jesus, I in my carnality cannot think I'm exempt from tribulations, and You who lived without sin had to die for sinners like myself. Through all of this, I'm letting go of my complaints, and I am lifting my hands in praise. Sorrows must bow as I surrender and experience mercy as only You can give. For now, I'll trust You, and when it's all over, I'll gladly testify of Your goodness. In Jesus' name, Amen.

## ❧Reflections❧

## ❧Personal Prayer❧

## This Week I've Seen God

## People To Pray For

## Week 41

*This I say then, Walk in the Spirit, and ye shall not fulfil the lust of the flesh.*
Galatians 5:16

Holy Spirit, prompt me clearly that I may respond to Your leadings. I desire to be guided by You in all of my dealings. There have been so many times I have gratified the cravings of my sinful nature with things opposed to God. I give up control, because when I give in to my sensual longings the end result is never good.

Enlighten me and show me the path I am to take that would please You, my guide. If I must return to the place of my failure in order to be corrected and to come to a pleasant place, I'll follow. Help me to rely on You as my inner witness. I know that You will not tell me anything contrary to Your Word.

Help me to be a follower of others on this trip in life that are one with You. I pray not to deceive or be deceived. Give me understanding of Your Word, that I totally lean on Your wisdom. Cause any course of action that I take to be one that goes only in the direction that You give me to take.

Give me a keen sensitive ear that will lead me to obey You. Speak to my heart and warn me of danger and help me rely on You as my place of refuge. Holy Spirit, in my own strength I cannot submit to You, I cry out to You for help that only You can give.

I do not want to fulfill my fleshy lusts. In me there is no good thing apart from You. Be my reminder lest I forget that Your ways are always holy, right, and just. In Your mercy, I seek Your forgiveness for the times I've departed from Your way. Holy Spirit teach me how to live, how to be in unity with You, pleasing God. I need You and without You I have no purpose or sense of direction. Guide me Holy Spirit. In Jesus' name, Amen.

## ❧Reflections❧

## ❧Personal Prayer❧

## ❧This Week I've Seen God❧

## ❧People To Pray For❧

## Week 42

*I therefore, the prisoner of the Lord, beseech you that ye walk worthy of the vocation wherewith ye are called.*
*Ephesians 4:1 (KJV)*

God of peace and oneness, I come to You to answer the appeal to live a life that is worthy of Your divine calling. You call me to come to You and in doing so, there's a wide spectrum of work to engage in. There is the call to walk in the Spirit and in love. You call me to walk in unity and obedience to Your lifesaving commands.

Help me align my conduct, speech, and thoughts with all that You call me to be and do. Let Your call to walk in truth and with lips of praise reign in me daily. In answering Your call, You are seen in me, and that is ultimately the goal. Keep me away from discord and anything that would bring conflict between You and me or my fellow man. In obedience to Your Word, I can't walk worthy or in unity without putting forth the effort necessary to die to my selfish whims.

You pursue me, and I desire to be found and embraced by You so I can live in harmony with You. I want to be one that answers the call in a way that glorifies You. I desire to conduct myself as one resurrected from impure motives, sinfulness, pride and all the darkness of my unregenerated life.

Holy Spirit, You never give up on me. I refuse to give up on myself. Because You are abundantly able to cause Your grace to abound in my life, I know that You will give me sufficient grace to walk in a pleasing manner before you. The selfish desires that used to keep me in a state of deadness will fall away and die. I declare by faith that I will walk in humility, patience, gentleness, and forbearance with others. I will be a light that leads others to Christ. Your power is at work in me. I can love and obey You and no longer walk in divisiveness separated from You by my sins. Unify me with You in Jesus' name, Amen.

## ❧Reflections❧

## ❧Personal Prayer❧

## ❧ This Week I've Seen God ❧

## ❧ People To Pray For ❧

## Week 43

*Be careful for nothing; but in every thing by prayer and supplication with thanksgiving let your requests be made known unto God.*
*Philippians 4:6*

To the God that never slumbers or sleeps, I call out to You in my every circumstance with a heart of thanksgiving. When I fail to see my way, I will still cling to You and make my requests known to You. There is no dilemma too large for You. No door is open You can't close nor closed that You can't open. Trusting in You destroys the anxieties that come to taunt me. I am grateful to You no matter the challenges that come to the surface to catapult me into distress. My heart of thanksgiving places me into the center of Your perfect will.

I can bring You my concerns for something as vast as a national crisis or something as minute as the need for a convenient parking space. I'm grateful for Your comfort in trying days at work, reports from the doctor that overwhelm me, or even when my vehicle needs repair. Thanksgiving flows from within me when You give me a sister or brother to accompany me during times of weakness.

    Never do I desire to have a hardened heart. I don't want my heart to be darkened with foolishness. In all that I face, good or hard times, I have hope in You. I glorify You as the only True and Faithful God. I am continuously blessed because of Your generous heart of love. What You give me is more than anything this world has to give.

    I confess that there are times I am weary from sorrow and pain that seek to weigh me down and drown me in self-pity. I look back to your promises in scripture and see a multitude of reasons not to be anxious but truly thankful. Salvation and the sacrifice of Your life that atoned for my every sin gives me reason to praise You with all that's in me. In You is all I need to be whole, healed, and wholly victorious and liberated. To You, I bring all my requests and rest in Your power. Forever yours, Amen.

## ❧Reflections❧

## ❧Personal Prayer❧

## ❧This Week I've Seen God❧

_____
_____
_____
_____
_____
_____
_____
_____
_____

## ❧People To Pray For❧

_____
_____
_____
_____
_____
_____
_____
_____
_____
_____
_____
_____

## Week 44

*Set your affections on things above, not on things of the earth.*
Colossians 3:2

God of Renewal and Restoration, I need a touch from You on my mind. Things on this earth vie for my attention and at times cause me to not be as faithful as I desire. I know I'm on a journey home with You, and at times I become focused on these temporal things. Holy Spirit, I ask You to keep me reminded that I have the mind of Christ. Order my character, conduct, and conversation aright.

I know I can't run this race and be victorious if I don't keep my eyes focused on the eternal prize. The call to allow You to reign in my mind, heart, and attitude is a high call. Empower me to be valiant and answer the call. My life is hidden in You, and I want to be revived. I am confident that You won't call me to the treasures above without helping me to overcome obstacles that seek to hinder me from going forward in You.

Help me to keep a consistent mindset that's not easily defocused. Anything that seeks my devotion is idolatry, and I want nothing or anyone to sit upon the throne of my heart.

There are circumstances that seek to derail me and weigh me down with sins that so easily beset me, but I ask You to fight on my behalf that I may stand. Mold and remold me until I walk in ways pleasing to You. Prepare me to throw off these earthly carnal clothes and clothe myself with Your mercy, love, kindness, humility, forgiveness, and every possible attribute of Yours.

Help me to walk in peace knowing that I'll possess peace in its' fullness when I get home with You. I want to be so heavenly minded that the things of this earth do not cause me to desire them more than all of You. Keep me longing for the newness of my permanent home above. Increase my expectation of being with You eternally and living in pure holiness with my sisters and brothers in Christ. Forever God, Amen.

## ❧Reflections❧

## ❧Personal Prayer❧

## ❧This Week I've Seen God❧

## ❧People To Pray For❧

## Week 45

*In every thing give thanks: for this is the will of God in Christ Jesus concerning you.*
*1 Thessalonians 5:18*

Praise be to the God of Gods, the Master of ALL. I come to You in gladness with thanksgiving. I have been in and through much and defeat sought to take me under, but as I rise, I find nothing but reasons to thank You. My help has always come from You, and I trust in You completely. You are worthy of all praise.

Relationships have been broken up in my life, and I find myself thanking You because You never leave nor forsake me. There are times I can't see how I am going to make it financially, and I find myself thanking You for providing for me in ways I could not see. I bless and affectionately praise You for a good portion of my health. Whether I have to take medication or receive wholeness from Your very hand, I thank you.

Some of my actions and attitudes have held me in bondage, and out of nowhere, You provide me with liberty. The greatest most entangling bondage ever has been sin within me, and in Your love and grace, You gave me all of Yourself to free me. What could ever keep me from thanking You no matter what? You have never done anything to harm me. All that You've given me has come from Your love. I can't thank You enough.

Yes, Lord, there are times I get so caught up in my pain and times of weaknesses I forget to thank You. Please bear with me and know that my heart is always grateful. When my emotions are all over the place, I still love and thank You. I am Yours, and I am confident in Your love for me.

Even in my failures, I thank You for causing me to rise above or just for being with me through it all. I bless You with all that is within me. In those times, my lips don't express my gratefulness for who You are, bear with me Lord, and know that I AM THANKFUL TO YOU, Amen.

## Reflections

## Personal Prayer

## ❧ This Week I've Seen God ❧

---
---
---
---
---
---
---
---
---
---
---

## ❧ People To Pray For ❧

---
---
---
---
---
---
---
---
---
---
---
---
---

## Week 46

*And the grace of our Lord was exceeding abundant with faith and love which is in Christ Jesus.*
1 Timothy 1:14

Most generous and loving God, Your saving grace is too much for me to comprehend, but oh, how I am thankful for it. I am forever grateful that all my sinfulness has never been too much for the abundance of love You have for me. I daily experience Your grace in my everyday situations. I cannot even measure the ways You display Your redemption and deliverance, no matter the heights or depths of my mess.

I accept Your full pardon, Jesus. The weight of the cross and the depths of every nail struck in Your body overwhelm me when I think of all You gave for me. For me, You offered all of Yourself. Your gift is the most powerful and precious thing I've ever received in this world. There are times I live as though I take it all for granted. However, Lord, I know there is no other who would or could ever stand in my place and receive the penalty I should have received.

In ignorance and pure unbelief, I sinned against You outrageously, and You lavished me with grace. My lies didn't cause You to turn away or give up on me. My thievery, blasphemy, malicious intents, willfully knowingly being disobedient, shameful acts, and hypocrisy never caused You to disown me. I stand before You as one snatched out of the fire with the stench of all the smoke unable to hold my head up or move my limbs, but through charred lips and a scorched throat, I say, "Thank You!" for looking beyond my numerous faults. You saw and met my needs.

Oh, Father, in You, I find patience as I've never known. Your longsuffering is most welcomed in my life. From the very core of my being has the emptiness been filled. You, in Your excellence, have now nor ever will fail me. I desire to live the remainder of my days in Your care. I commend myself to You and the word of Your grace, which will surely build me up. I love and thank You, Lord, Amen.

## ❧Reflections❧

_____
_____
_____
_____
_____
_____
_____
_____
_____
_____

## ❧Personal Prayer❧

_____
_____
_____
_____
_____
_____
_____
_____
_____
_____
_____

## ≈This Week I've Seen God≈

## ≈People To Pray For≈

## Week 47

*To speak evil of no man, to be no brawlers, but gentle, showing all meekness unto all men.*
Titus 3:2

    Creative Father, the One who spoke the world into existence, oh how I long to use my tongue to praise You and uplift mankind. I see in Your Word Your commands to speak no evil of man nor words that would give the enemy a foothold in Your people's lives, and I fail many times. With a heart of pure repentance, I seek Your forgiveness, Lord.

    Thank You for the creative power of Your Word. Holy Spirit, empower me not to speak words that bring death to our lives or circumstances. Cause my lips to speak productive life-giving words. Help me to see the fruit of God's Word being manifest in every area of my life and the lives of those I cross paths with. Let the words that I speak align themselves with Your Word and birth faith in the midst of all I encounter. Give me faith that stands on Your

Word and prospers in the midst of any trial or tribulation. You've told me that I will be accountable for every word I speak. I desire justification for my words and not condemnation. You've given us the power to bind and loose on this earth and the effects will reach heaven; so I bind up every idle word I've ever spoken, every self-imposed curse and every curse spoken by me against others or spoken against me by others in Jesus powerful matchless name. Your Word shall not return to you void but will accomplish what You please and prosper in the thing You send it to. I decree and declare that my mouth will be satisfied with good things so that my youth is renewed like the eagles. I now speak words of life and not death.

I reject curses that I may have spoken over others. Father, I pray that through the power of the Holy Spirit You destroy the effects of every idle destructive word I've ever spoken.

Empowered by the truth of Your Word, I now speak words of encouragement, blessings, faith, love, mercy, and life. I look forward to being a verbal channel of blessings on Your behalf. In Jesus' name, Amen.

## ❧Reflections❧

## ❧Personal Prayer❧

## ~This Week I've Seen God~

## ~People To Pray For~

## Week 48

*So that we may boldly say, The Lord is My Helper, and I will not fear what man shall do unto me.*
*Hebrews 13:6*

Trusting Savior, because I am united with You, I am able to make bold declarations based on Your character. In You, I find rest and no reason to be seized with alarm. Fear can't overwhelm me any longer. I choose to trust Your voice and not the loud screams of doubt that seek to derail me. I am Yours and You are the capable loving Shepherd of the flock.

The taunts of others desiring to make me flee like a coward no longer trouble me. I look into the light of Your Word and am comforted. My mind no longer runs to and fro so rampantly. I am still and resting in the refuge only You offer. You are the reason I'm bold in the face of adversity and turn obstacles into opportunities. With You as my helper, I overcome all things in Your power. You are my strength, song, and salvation. I am never alone because of Your

Presence. I love that I am a part of Your Body. There are sisters and brothers that You place in my path to show me the path to take and walk with me on this journey.

I can't count the times You've placed a blessed partner to assure me that I can look to You for help. I've come to know Your Presence when two or more of my spiritual siblings gathered as one. You've been a constant in my life. The tie that binds me to helpers in storms is You. In Your name, we have put many adversaries to fright.

I am not afraid of the tactics of man, for they are no match for You. I walk in You and You've never been defeated. I stand face to face with any giant because Lord You are the object of my faith. There are many heavenly witnesses who have told of their challenges in the Bible. Regardless of the turbulence, they come out victoriously. I trust I will too. In Jesus' name, Amen.

## ❧Reflections❧

## ❧Personal Prayer❧

## ❧This Week I've Seen God❧

## ❧People To Pray For❧

## Week 49

*But be ye doers of the Word, and not hearers only, deceiving your own selves.*
James 1:22

Wonderful Counselor, to You I run rapidly seeking Your power to change my heart and cause me to love Your Word enough to walk in obedience. Breathe on me and lead me in the way of truth and holiness. Let me be intimately acquainted with Your Word and die to any desire to go in opposition to it. If You say I can do it, You give me the power to walk into the reality of every command. I never want to live contrary to the Truth.

Open the ears of my heart that I'll know the difference between falsehoods and verity. Equip me to mortify the deeds of my flesh. No longer do I want to answer my carnality. I've fallen enough and I rise with the help of You, the Lifter of My Soul. Freedom from my old self is in You, and I do arise. I wake up from the deadness of deception and every form of disobedience. No longer do I doubt the power of the Holy Spirit for me. Yes, You're available for me. I can make it. Victory does belong to me.

Open the ears of my heart to hear Your voice and follow any command You give. Instruct me in the ways of holiness. Purify me. I come to You as is yet abandoning myself to Your complete control. In dying I actually find life. Change me inwardly until the fruit of newness is displayed wholly.

You didn't create me to be defeated, but to be more than a conqueror. I bow at Your feet and give You all of me trusting You to reign in me. I want to please You with more than mere formalities. Obedience is always better than sacrifice. To You, I give my will and rejoice in being a new creature where old things are passed away all things in me are new. I thank You, my Savior. In Jesus' name, Amen.

## Reflections

## Personal Prayer

## ❧This Week I've Seen God❧

## ❧People To Pray For❧

## Week 50

*Being born again, not of corruptible seed, but of incorruptible; by the Word of God, which liveth and abideth forever.*
1 Peter 1:23

Regenerator of my soul, I am filled with an abundance of gratitude for Your gift of salvation. Hallelujah, I am truly born again because of the gracious sacrifice of Jesus Christ. No one can take what You've given me. I am actually holy. Who would have ever guessed that a sinful creature as myself could be adopted into the Royal Family? Forever will I be thankful.

What You've done for me, no other person was qualified to do. I am pure and my sins have been washed away by Your own blood. I have access to You and do not have to go through another. You have shone Your light of love in every dark corner of my heart. Every breath I take is because of You. All my hope is rooted and grounded in You.

I am born again! I am governed by Your Holy Spirit. All my praise belongs to You. No longer am I in a weak, beggarly, impoverished state. You have taken the lump of dishonorable clay that I was and shaped me into a vessel of honor. The work You have begun is not in vain and will continue until Your return when it will be complete. The work You have done is incorruptible and no man can ever take credit for it.

By grace through the channel of faith, I am renewed. The deadness in me is now alive. The brokenness in me has been mended. The ruins of my life have been restored. I look to You always for help and guidance on this new journey. I can't say I know how to live, but I am glad You have never left me nor ever will.

Again, Lord, I thank You for giving me this new life. I was blind, now I see. I was deaf, now I hear. I had a hard heart, now I have a heart of flesh. Who can I thank but You? I am forever grateful. In Jesus' powerful, life-changing name, Amen.

## ❧Reflections❧

## ❧Personal Prayer❧

## ❧This Week I've Seen God❧

## ❧People To Pray For❧

## Week 51

*Ye are of God, little children, and have overcome them: because greater is He that is in you, than he that is in the world.*
1 John 4:4

Victorious God, I praise You to the highest degree I can because I have all that You possess today. No longer must I wallow in all the pains of my past. Your greatness exceeds my wrongs and I am able to claim Your victory and Your supernatural power.

I am Yours and that truth enables me to run my race in peace. Your love comforts and sustains me. To belong to You gives me strength to stand against all that rise to oppose me and cause me to be weak and wounded. I face the world today and all the imps of the adversary in Your might.

Your peace overrides my chaos. Your wisdom supersedes my intellect. Your presence within me pushes my dismay and fears out of my path.

In every part of me that wants to believe I'm an outcast with no place to go, You have become my refuge. The life of God in me resurrects me from all the bondage I've placed myself in. I have grown in leaps and bounds as I have experienced Your love and mercy. Not once have You failed me nor left me in a battle alone. It amazes me how You've pursued me with Your love. I can't count the times I've known Your embrace, sometimes running and kicking. You have never left me alone.

   I dare to be a courageous, bold warrior today and share the truth of who You are. Today I want to encourage a lone sojourner to stop chasing emptiness and vanity and run into the arms of You – REAL LOVE and POWER! No longer do we have to be hopeless because to be one with You is to defeat any challenge that comes against us. In any weakness we encounter, we can welcome Your overwhelming strength. You in us is greater than anything the world brings our way. We are in a fixed fight – in Christ, we are always victorious. Thank you. In Jesus' name, Amen.

## ❧Reflections❧

_____
_____
_____
_____
_____
_____
_____
_____
_____
_____
_____

## ❧Personal Prayer❧

_____
_____
_____
_____
_____
_____
_____
_____
_____
_____
_____

## ≫This Week I've Seen God≪

## ≫People To Pray For≪

> ## *Week 52*

*He which testifieth these things saith, Surely I come quickly. Amen. Even so, come, Lord Jesus.*
*Revelation 22:20*

    Returning and Reigning Lord and Savior, I welcome You. The mere fact that I will see my Risen Savior's face bring immeasurable joy to the depths of my soul. To live with You forever takes my breath away. I can't say how I will react, but my response will be brimming with gratitude. I thank You, Jesus, for Your departure from heaven. Your arrival and stay on earth couples with Your savage crucifixion and spectacular resurrection have kept us for numerous years; however, the gift of immortality in Your presence is the ultimate wrapping of it all. I do cry from the core of my being, come Lord Jesus, come.

    Eternal shouts of praise will come from me for Your joy turning all my sadness upside down.

There will be no more tears, no ailments, no hunger or thirst or even scorching heat. You the Lamb of God will forever prevail and overcome all the death and darkness of our greatest enemy – Satan. No longer will we have to fear any of his tactics. All doubt will be washed away. We will experience You beyond limitations of this earthly realm.

The Living Word Himself will walk and talk to us face to face. Where else would we rather be than with You eternal? Come, the One who was clothed in patience and mercy unfathomable while we were adorned in our earthly tents. No longer shall we cry out, "Where are You?" We will enjoy moment by moment with You. You will be the forever shining Son in our lives.

The Shepherd of our Souls will forever guide us to springs of continual flowing waters of life. The pastures will be lush and green, full of all the nourishment we need. I await the day I see You come from the clouds You ascended to years ago. My heart cries out louder and louder, "Come quickly Lord, even so come quickly."

I await Your coming. Praise Your Holy Name, Amen.

## ❧Reflections❧

## ❧Personal Prayer❧

## This Week I've Seen God

## People To Pray For

## About the Author

*Jennifer Kelly* is a mother of three wonderful children and two golden grandchildren. This is Jennifer's first book written from the heart as a Georgia prison inmate to encourage others to find the hope and healing only God can provide through redemption. She is a fervent prayer warrior, encourager, and woman of faith. Connect with Jennifer Kelly at jk883504@gmail.com.

Jennifer Kelly's prison intake photo.

Made in the USA
Columbia, SC
19 March 2020